FUNCTIONAL PROGRAMMING:
Languages, Tools and Architectures

ELLIS HORWOOD BOOKS IN COMPUTING SCIENCE

General Editors: Professor JOHN CAMPBELL, University College London, and BRIAN L. MEEK, King's College London (KQC), University of London

Series in Computers and their Applications
Series Editor: BRIAN L. MEEK, Computer Centre, King's College London (KQC), University of London

An up-to-date and readable list of texts on the theory and practice of computing, with the emphasis on computer applications and new or developing areas: a valuable nucleus for all computing science libraries and departments.

Series in Computer Communications and Networking
Series Editor: R. J. DEASINGTON, International Computers Limited (UK), Edinburgh

Books covering an area of growing current interest in data communications technology, local area networks (LANs) and wide area networks (WANs); aimed at both professional users of network and communication systems, as well as academics.

Series in Artificial Intelligence
Series Editor: Professor JOHN CAMPBELL, University College London

Books which reflect the latest and most important developments in the field of Artificial Intelligence, edited by a most prestigious and well respected authority of world renown.

Series in Cognitive Science
Series Editor: MASOUD YAZDANI, Department of Computer Science, University of Exeter

A series which reports on work being carried out in an emerging discipline, an area of articial intelligence which is being recognised as an independent study in its own right.

ELLIS HORWOOD BOOKS IN INFORMATION TECHNOLOGY

General Editor: Dr JOHN M. M. PINKERTON, Principal, McLean Pinkerton Associates, Surrey (formerly General Manager of Strategic Requirements, ICL)

Books are planned in this area in knowledge engineering, expert systems, the human-computer interface, computational linguistics; and will cover the many applications of information technology

If you would like more information on titles in any of these areas, please contact our distributors and ask them for a catalogue of our publications.

JOHN WILEY & SONS LTD
Baffins Lane
Chichester
West Sussex
England

Halsted Press: a division of
JOHN WILEY & SONS, INC
605 Third Avenue
New York, NY 10158
USA

FUNCTIONAL PROGRAMMING:
Languages, Tools and Architectures

Editor:

S. EISENBACH, B.A., M.Sc.
Lecturer, Department of Computing
Imperial College of Science & Technology, London

ELLIS HORWOOD LIMITED
Publishers · Chichester

Halsted Press: a division of
JOHN WILEY & SONS
New York · Chichester · Brisbane · Toronto

First published in 1987 by
ELLIS HORWOOD LIMITED
Market Cross House, Cooper Street,
Chichester, West Sussex, PO19 1EB, England
The publisher's colophon is reproduced from James Gillison's drawing of the ancient Market Cross, Chichester.

Distributors:

Australia and New Zealand:
JACARANDA WILEY LIMITED
GPO Box 859, Brisbane, Queensland 4001, Australia

Canada:
JOHN WILEY & SONS CANADA LIMITED
22 Worcester Road, Rexdale, Ontario, Canada

Europe and Africa:
JOHN WILEY & SONS LIMITED
Baffins Lane, Chichester, West Sussex, England

North and South America and the rest of the world:
Halsted Press: a division of
JOHN WILEY & SONS
605 Third Avenue, New York, NY 10158, USA

British Library Cataloguing in Publication Data
Functional programming: languages, tools and architectures. —
(Ellis Horwood series in computers and their applications)
1. Electronic digital computers — Programming
I. Eisenbach, S.
005.1   QA76.6

Library of Congress Card No. 86–10528

ISBN 0–85312–973–8 (Ellis Horwood Limited)
ISBN 0–470–20391–9 (Halsted Press)

Printed in Great Britain by Unwin Bros. Woking

Contents

To Chris who waited while I worked on the ALICE book.

Preface

conclusion

Functional programming has been gaining popularity for three reasons. Firstly there is the conciseness of the programming languages that allow programmers to write shorter more elegant programs than in conventional languages. Secondly there is the amenability to mathematical analysis that enables programmers to write programs that look like specifications and automatic transformation systems to convert them to efficient running programs. And finally functional programs can easily exploit the parallelism of multi-processor machines.

This book is divided into three parts which respectively cover language, theory and architecture. Chris Sadler and I have written an overview chapter on functional programming; Roger Bailey describes one functional programming language, Hope, in detail; John Darlington explains what program transformation is and how it's a powerful method for developing correct and efficient programs from their specifications; and Martin Cripps, Tony Field and Mike Reeve describe ALICE, a highly parallel machine that was designed to execute functional programs.

The rest of the programming section contains two functional programming alternatives to Hope. For programmers who prefer an APL like syntax, Peter Harrison and Hessam Khoshnevisan describe FP, a language designed by John Backus. Finally, for programmers who cannot get access to a functional language programming system (or for programmers who want to feel what the functional programming paradigm feels like before they make the effort to get a functional language translator), Roger Bailey shows how to write functional programs in Pascal syntax.

Peter Harrison and Hessam Khoshnevisan describe an algebraic approach to reasoning about FP programs. Ian Moor describes how to write large programs in a functional programming style.

It is difficult to get functional programs to run efficiently on conventional computers and the architecture section contains chapters on four alternatives suitable for executing functional programs. Besides the description of ALICE, there is also a chapter by Chris Hankin, David Till and Hugh Glaser on how another design of parallel machine, called data flow, could support functional programming. Brian Boutel describes another architecture called combinators and Lee McLoughlin and I describe still another architecture called Ruth that seem suitable for implementing functional programming languages. Combinators and Ruth can either be used as emulators on conventional machines to enable functional programs to be translated or implemented as hardware.

Some of the authors have assumed other chapters have been read prior to reading their chapter. For any reader with no previous knowledge about functional programming, Chapter 1 is a prerequisite for every other chapter. Chapter 2 is a prerequisite for all the chapters in the architecture part, as well as for Chapter 5 and Chapter 7. Chapter 3 and Chapter 8 are prerequisites for Chapter 6, which also requires a good mathematical background.

There is much research into functional programming at several universities. Although ideas are similar concrete syntax varies from place to place. The chapters in this book were written mainly by people in the Declarative Language Architecture section of Imperial College's Department of Computing. Apologies to ML and Miranda users who will not find their favourite syntax described here. The authors not from Imperial College are David Till from Kings College, London, Chris Sadler from the Polytechnic of North London and Brian Boutel from Victoria University at Wellington (on leave at Imperial College when he wrote his chapter).

This book is aimed at computer professionals and computer science undergraduates who would like to learn about functional programming. I would like to thank Phil Lemmons of *Byte Magazine* and who had the courage to commission many of the chapters and Thomas Clune for his help in editing. Some of the material in Chapters 1, 2, 3, 5, 6 and 9 first appeared in *Byte* in a slightly different form. I would also like to thank Ian Moor for his help in producing the bibliography and Simon Brock for producing the programs.

Susan Eisenbach
Imperial College, January 1987

1

Why Functional Programming?

Chris Sadler and Susan Eisenbach

There are literally hundreds of programming languages. Some are designed to get the optimum performance out of the systems they run on regardless of the amount of time it takes to produce the program. Others are designed to enhance programmer productivity, usually at the expense of efficient use of machine-time. Some are special-purpose languages, designed to be applicable only to a restricted range of problems, while others attempt a jack-of-all-trades approach by offering features applicable to a variety of different problem types.

As time goes by, the expanding scope and complexity of problems tackled by computers together with the advances of technology, mean that programming languages tend to exhibit something akin to evolutionary behaviour, with some becoming extinct, some new ones emerging and some adapting and surviving. Underpinning this creation and adaptation of programming languages however, there have been developments in our understanding of the activities of problem-solving and programming, and changes in our conception both of language and of machine-'intelligence'. These theoretical considerations have had the effect of founding families of languages (continuing the evolutionary analogy) so that most languages can trace a 'parentage' back to one or more original ideas. This book is about one such family, known as the *functional* languages, which has long been highly regarded in academic circles, being eminently problem-oriented but extremely inefficient computationally. The 'fifth generation' hardware makes it look as though the functional family may be entering its own era.

HARDWARE PROBLEMS

Virtually all computers are architecturally equivalent to the first machines built in the 1940s. They have one central processor (CPU) connected to a relatively large passive memory by a bus which is one word wide. Eventually after much tuning of the software and several hardware upgrades most systems become 'processor bound' when the CPU itself isn't fast enough to cope with the tasks it is supposed to perform. At this stage a new computer is normally obtained, with the same basic architecture but faster components. Every breakthrough in hardware technology leads to improvements in speed which raise the expectations of users which can only be met by another technological breakthrough. There are not many turns left through this cycle before we hit some natural barrier (like the speed of light) which closes off the line of development.

One way out of this cul-de-sac lies in an examination of the justification behind the conventional machine architecture. The ratio between processor cost and memory cost used to be extremely high since processors were expensive, requiring many boards of components. This is no longer the case — both processors and memory are made from the same technology (LSI and VLSI) and in practice, it is only the smallest microcomputer systems that don't have additional, special-purpose processors to deal with storage, input–output peripherals, floating point operations and so on, although there is still only a single central processing unit. For applications that require higher throughput it makes sense to try to build machines out of networks of more general-purpose processors each of which can take a share of the processing load.

Many users who require substantial processing power have programs containing large arrays of data (meteorology, oil exploration, defence problems). So one kind of parallel machine consists of an array of processors which simultaneously obey the same instructions. A very high throughput can be achieved if the user's problem can be written so that there are arrays whose elements all need the same operations performed on them. Another more flexible system consists of a 'pipeline' of processors, each of which performs a portion of the calculation on each piece of data before passing its results on to the next processor down the line. Unfortunately, it is quite difficult to exploit this 'lock-step' parallelism since not all problems are easily cast into a suitable form.

The next alternative is to use languages which explicitly control the parallel execution of processes. Languages such as Modula-2 and Ada have constructs that allow the programmer to initiate and coordinate multiple concurrent tasks. Typically, these share a single processor but there is no reason why parallel processors could not be used, especially when there are a few tasks, possibly even tens of tasks. This becomes less practical when the count of simultaneous tasks may run to thousands.

Just as the languages we conventionally use mirror conventional architecture (that is, they are sequential in nature), in order to take full advantage of parallel processing systems, we need a type of language in which it is natural to describe complex problems in such a way that they can be (automatically) solved concurrently. One can then gain arbitrary increases in speed simply by adding more processors.

SOFTWARE PROBLEMS

Much research has gone into improving programmer productivity, especially when it was found that the costs of employing teams of programmers began to outweigh the costs of purchasing and maintaining the computers they were using. Two startling findings have made quite a difference to the way things have developed on the software front. The first of these is the fact that, whatever programming language is used, any given programmer produces roughly the same number of lines of code (written, tested, debugged and documented). The implication of this finding is that the more powerful the language is (that is, the more computing that can be encompassed in each construct, rather than simply the number of different constructs available to the programmer), the more productive that programmer becomes, and so over the years there has been a trend towards higher-level programming languages. (For the record, the average output for a professional programmer is around 1500 lines per year — although individuals vary widely in their own capabilities.)

A second trend follows from an analysis of those elements within programs which appear to be particularly prone to error and their elimination in new language definitions. This has the effect of limiting the control which can be exercised over the machine at the programmer's whim. The first step in this direction occurred with the move from assembly languages to the original high level languages. Instead of laying the whole of available memory open to the programmer, to access and interpret in any way (or variety of ways) desired, the programmer was constrained to naming storage locations (*variables*) and to declaring the type of data that would be stored there. This step simultaneously restricts the freedom of the programmer to manoeuvre around the data and imposes a layer of organisation (structure) on the data (and hence the program).

The next element to come under the scrutiny of the language designers was the infamous GOTO statement which seemed to crop up time and again embedded in the more horrendous programming errors. The elimination of GOTO statements gave rise to structured programming in which programs are built up by means of a set of well-defined constructs guaranteed to ensure a rational and predictable flow of control. Another feature on the blacklist was global data with its insidious side effects. A new style of programming was developed — modular programming, which restricts programmers to working on small manageable sub-problems and passing all data explicitly between modules. When a problem arises the offending module can be identified and the effects of the error rapidly traced.

Both structured and modular programming philosophies lend themselves to an improved correspondence between the specification of a problem (a concise but exhaustive statement of what the program will be expected to do, under all circumstances) and the program's final realisation (the code running on a given hardware configuration). Nevertheless this correspondence is usually not rigorous in the sense that no one tends to take the trouble to go through the program actually proving that each module does its job correctly and then passes its results to the right receiving modules in the correct form (even though painstaking mathematical techniques generally exist to do this).

The second finding to come out of the research into programmer productivity is that, in the average commercial programming environment, as much as 50% of programmer effort goes into program maintenance — that is, updating the program's performance to meet circumstances not envisaged when the program was originally specified, or hunting for deep-seated bugs. Since deep-seated bugs are simply places where the program, as written, diverges from its original specification (if one was ever produced), a major improvement in efficiency can be gained from improving the precision of program specifications and from tying the program more tightly to its specification. Note that if no specification was produced initially, then the maintenance programmer has to try to deduce what was intended by examining code which is known to be incorrect.

Making a specification more precise means searching for ways to make unambiguous statements about what the program should achieve, and the most unambiguous language is the language of mathematics, so the trend has been towards more mathematical (and provable) methods of description. By the same token, tying program code to specification implies not only a trend towards still higher-level languages but also towards the use of mathematical methods of proof applied to actual fragments of code. This serves both to demonstrate that the code will have a predictable outcome under all circumstances (rather than those circumstances selected experimentally during 'testing') and that the outcomes match those called for in the specification.

One noteworthy barrier which prevents the programmer from using reasonably straightforward mathematics for exploring possible solutions to a problem or for testing existing code, is the familiar assignment operation. Programmers use the word 'variable' to refer to a named storage location whose value (contents) can be modified by means of assignment statements. Therefore, in order to know what such a variable 'stands for' it is necessary to know precisely at which point in the program's execution the enquiry is being made — and each variable has a 'computational history' which charts its changing values for the lifetime of the program. By contrast, if a mathematical variable exists, it has a value and if that value has not yet been computed, then the variable is simply unknown — it is not some other value. This property is known as *referential transparency*.

In order to make a piece of code amenable to mathematical analysis, it is necessary to free variables from the burden of their computational histories — which means restricting the extent to which programmers may assign values to a variable. Languages with referential transparency are known as *declarative languages* because, without assignments, programmers can only declare what effects should produce what outcomes; by contrast, *'imperative languages'* require the programmer to prescribe the manner and especially the sequence in which processing should occur. Functional (or sometimes applicative) languages are declarative whose fundamental computational component is the *function*, (to stress the importance of function application). Declarative languages, where the *relation* is the fundamental unit, are generally termed logic languages but are beyond the scope of this book.

Apart from stabilising variables so that finite mathematical techniques can be applied to code fragments, referential transparency serves to remove the flow mechanisms (specifically sequencing and loops) from explicit mention in the code. This in turn allows for the possibility of parallel processing: since any function in a program can be executed whenever all its parameters are defined (rather than when the programmer decides that the CPU is available for this purpose), there is no reason why a program cannot be spread over a collection of processors so that each function can get its own processor or share one with a small subset of the whole program.

However referential transparency has other implications for functional languages. Since the unknown variables in any expression are simply unevaluated function calls, which become known as the function code is executed, one effect is to blur the distinction between functions (code) and variables (data). This leads to the idea of *higher-order functions*. These functions are capable of accepting as arguments and also of returning, other first and higher-order functions so that the programmer can structure and manipulate functions and data with equal facility. Secondly, static data structures like arrays necessarily have computational histories and so must be replaced in functional languages by dynamic data structures where memory for an item is allocated only when that item comes into existence. Some imperative languages like Pascal and C implement dynamic data structures rather primitively by means of *pointers* which require the programmer to reference memory locations explicitly. In functional languages dynamic structures are treated in more abstract terms (for example, as *lists*). Lists serve to bring code and data together even more closely since they incorporate implicit operations (or 'functions') for including components in the structure (*constructors*) and for extracting components from the structure (*selectors*). What follows is a brief description of a representative sample of languages, showing some of the differences in approach, in mathematical paradigms and of course in syntax.

PURE LISP

LISP stands for LISt Processing. It is by far the oldest of the functional languages having been designed by John McCarthy of MIT in 1960. Numerous imperative features have been added to different versions of the language so that most Lisp programs are not actually declarative, but there is a large enough subset (Pure Lisp) to allow functional programming to be done (e.g. Peter Henderson of Stirling University's system called Lispkit). Lisp has more different dialects than any other functional language, and since it is the most mature of the functional languages there is a large range of software tools as well as custom-designed hardware. MIT's Maclisp will be used in the programming example.

Data structures in a Lisp program are constructed from atoms, where an atom is either a numeral or a literal string. Although some Lisps have other data structures, the only standard data structure is the list. Lists need not contain homogeneous elements as Lisp is an untyped language (types are actually determined at run-time.). For example

```
( A 1 (ABC 123) )
```

is a list containing three elements. Since there is only one data structure, access methods have been built into the language. Thus there are selector functions (car and cdr); constructor functions (list and cons); and a predicate (null) whether a list is empty.

Not only is a Lisp data structure a list but programs are lists as well. Therefore a list can be executed and will return a value or it can be used as an argument for another program. Higher-order functions are implemented through a device called the lambda expression which enables a Lisp programmer to define and manipulate functions as data objects. The basic unit of a Lisp program is the expression (compared to the statement in most imperative languages) and every Lisp construct computes a value. Recursion is the only control mechanism.

As an example of a Lisp program, the following function will calculate the length of a list, l:

```
( defun length ( l )
    ( cond (( null l) 0 )
          ( t ( add1( length( cdr l ) ) ) ) )
    )
)
```

This program works on a list where each element can be of any type. In English it says

> Length is a function which takes list as its only argument. If the list is empty then the number zero is returned; otherwise (represented by the 't') the length of the list is one more than the length of the list without the first element.

FP

FP stands for Functional Programming. The language was designed by John Backus of IBM and described in his Turing Award lecture in 1977 (he was being awarded for his other contributions to computer science — Fortran and BNF). At first glance FP shows the influence of APL in its syntax ('APL without variables').

Backus's claim is that programmers tend to manipulate data rather than functions, starting with input data and putting this through a series of functions until the required output data is reached. In the FP style of programming, primitive functions are combined in such a way as to produce a final function (the program). This is then applied to the input data to produce the output — hence no variables are required.

FP programs map single objects onto each other where a single object is either an atom (an integer or finite string of upper case letters) or a sequence of atoms. FP's atoms and sequences are comparable to Lisp's atoms and lists. Primitive functions provided by FP include arithmetic and sequence operations, a set of predicates and APL's iota operator for producing the first n integers.

There are several ways of combining functions (the *combining forms*). These are:

(1) composition — written as $f°g$
Given two functions f and g, $f°g$ is the function obtained by first applying g to the argument of the function and taking the result of this function as the argument of f.

(2) construction — written as $[f_1, f_2 \ldots, f_n]$
Creating a sequence of *n* elements whose ith element is obtained by applying f_i to the input data.

(3) conditional — written as $p \rightarrow f;g$
If the predicate p is true apply f to the argument and if p is false apply g.

(4) apply to all — written as αf
Create a sequence of the same length as the input sequence by applying f to each element of the input data.

(5) insert — written as $/f$
Apply f to the sequence formed by the first element of the input data followed by $/f$ applied to the rest of the input sequence.

The FP style of programming is not explicitly recursive like the other functional languages because recursion is implicit within the combining forms.

As an example of an FP program, the following returns the length of a list:

$$\textbf{def } \text{length} = /+°\alpha \ \overline{1}$$

This program works on a sequence where each element can be of any type. Notice that there are no variables. In English it says

Treat each element of the sequence as a 1 and add them up.

HOPE

Hope (named after Hope Park Square, home of Edinburgh's Department of Computer Science) was designed by Dave MacQueen (Bell Labs), Rod Burstall and Don Sannella (Edinburgh) and is one of several *recursion equation* languages. In these, each function is represented by a set of equations which together will provide a result for the whole range of function arguments; a program is simply a hierarchy of these functions, together with a single invocation of the highest level function.

Hope allows the programmer to define specific or polymorphic data types which are checked by the compiler. Polymorphic types allow for the creation of functions that can be applied to more than one type of data (for instance a routine that can sort numbers, characters, strings or records). The data types *num* (positive integer), *truval* (boolean), *char*, *list* and *set* are predefined and these can be used to build up more sophisticated data structures by means of type variables and data statements.

The LISP program uses the conditional cond to distinguish between alternative forms of a list (i.e., an empty list or a nonempty list). In Hope the two cases are represented explicitly (rather than symbolically) by *patterns* (nil and First :: RestOfList respectively). Instead of using the conditional, the program is expected to make the appropriate selection by *matching* the actual list against the possible patterns.

To solve a problem using Hope the programmer designs data structures that match the problem; derives higher-order functions (like FP's combining forms) to traverse these data structures and then invokes the higher-order functions with arguments which represent instances for which specific results are required.

Finally, Hope has a modular structure. Thus, a programmer can implement an abstract data type (e.g. a queue) with a type declaration and a collection of functions to operate on that type. The implementation of these functions and the representation of the type itself can be hidden from the user, who relies solely on the specified properties of the abstract type.

As an example of a Hope program, the following computes the length of a list:

```
dec length : list( alpha ) -> num
--- length( nil ) <= 0
--- length( First :: RestOfList ) <= 1 + length
                                        (RestOfList)
```

This program works on a list where the elements are all of the same unspecified type. In English it says

> Length is a function which takes a list of type 'alpha' and returns a number. If the list is empty then the number returned is zero; otherwise the length of the list is one more than the length of the list without the first element.

CONCLUSION

The key to the solution of some of our hardware and software problems seems to lie in incorporating the referential transparency enjoyed by mathematical variables into the design of (functional) programming languages. This course of action appears

(i) to improve the coupling between compilable source code and the abstractions of a specification language; (see Part I)

(ii) to make the code amenable to direct mathematical verification; (see Part II)

(iii) to open up a way to perform true parallel processing; (see Part III)

(iv) to bring code and data conceptually closer together; (see Part I)

(v) to permit the implementation of polymorphic abstract data types. (see Part I)

Part I
Languages

An Introduction to Hope

Roger Bailey

FUNCTIONS IN CONVENTIONAL LANGUAGES

In a language like Pascal, a function is a piece of 'packaged' program for performing standard operations like finding square roots. To obtain the square root of a positive number stored in a variable x, we write:

```
sqrt ( x )
```

at the point in the program where the value is required, such as:

```
writeln ( 1.0 + sqrt ( x ) ) ;
```

this is called an *application* of the function. The value represented by x is called the *argument* or *actual parameter*. In this context, the 'packaged' program computes the square root of x, 1.0 is added to it and the result is printed.

We may define our own functions, specifying how the result is computed by means of ordinary Pascal statements. The following function delivers the greater of its two argument values:

```
function max ( x, y : INTEGER ) : INTEGER ;
begin
if x > y
    then max := x
    else max := y
end ;
```

The identifiers x and y are called *formal parameters*. They are used inside the body to name the two values which will be supplied as arguments when the function is applied. max can be used anywhere a value is needed, just like sqrt; here it is used to filter out negative values on output:

```
writeln ( max ( z, 0 ) ) ;
```

A more interesting case is when the actual parameter is a function application itself or involves one. `max` can be used to find the largest of *three* numbers by writing:

```
max ( a, max ( b, c ) )
```

Combining function applications like this is called *composition*. The expression is evaluated 'inside-out' because the outer application of `max` cannot be evaluated until the value of its second argument is known. The *inner* application of `max` is therefore evaluated first using the values of b and c and the result is used as the actual parameter of the outer application.

Functions may also be combined by using simple ones as 'building blocks' to define more powerful ones. If it were frequently required to find the largest of three numbers, it might be more convenient to define:

```
function MaxOfThree ( x, y, z : INTEGER ) : INTEGER ;
begin
MaxOfThree := max ( x, max ( y, z ) )
end ;
```

and apply it by writing:

```
MaxOfThree ( a, b, c )
```

PROGRAMMING WITH FUNCTIONS

Pascal is an *imperative* language because programs written in it are recipes for 'doing something'. When programs are written using functions, it becomes possible to concentrate on *what* the results are and largely to ignore *how* they are computed. We can forget that `sqrt` is a piece of code and simply think of `sqrt ( x )` as a way of writing a *value* in a program. `MaxOfThree` can be treated the same way if we ignore the way it works inside. By defining a 'toolkit' of useful functions and combining them together like this, it is possible to build powerful programs which are quite short and easy to understand.

In Pascal, functions can deliver only 'simple' data objects such as numbers or characters, but significant programs need data structures and cannot easily be written using this limited kind of function. In Hope, a function may deliver *any* type of value, including data structures equivalent to the **array** and **record** of Pascal and much more. Programming in Hope has the flavour of simply 'writing down the answer' by writing an expression which defines it. This will contain one or more function applications to define smaller parts of the answer. These functions will not usually be built in like `sqrt`, and must be defined by the programmer, but they can still be thought of as *definitions* of data objects, and not as *algorithms* for computing them.

A SIMPLE HOPE EXAMPLE—CONDITIONALS

We will consider the definition of `max` in Hope. Like Pascal, Hope is a *strongly-typed* language, which means that the compiler must be informed about the types of all objects in the program so it can check that they are used consistently. The function definition comes in two parts. First the types of the arguments and the result are declared:

```
dec max : num # num -> num ;
```

dec is a reserved word (in lower case), and may not be used as a name. max is the name of the function being defined. Names consist of upper and lower case letters (which are distinct) and digits, and must start with a letter. The layout is not significant and symbols may be separated by any number of blanks, tabs and newlines for clarity, as in this example. Adjacent symbols need only be separated when they might otherwise be confused as one, such as dec and max.

The next part of the declaration gives the types of the arguments (the symbol : is read as 'takes a'). Non-negative integers are of the predefined type num (in lower case). # is read as 'and a' (the reserved word X can be used instead). -> is read as 'yields'. The semicolon marks the end of the declaration, which informs the compiler that max takes two numbers as arguments and delivers a single number as its result.

The result of a function is defined by one or more *recursion equations*. max needs only a single equation:

```
--- max ( x, y ) <=  if x > y then x else y ;
```

The symbol --- is read as 'the value of'. The expression max (x, y) is called the *left-hand side* of the equation and defines x and y as formal parameters, or local names for the values which will be supplied when the function is applied. Parameter names are local to the equation, so x and y will not be confused with any other x or y in the program. The symbol <= is read as 'is defined as'.

The rest of the equation (called the *right-hand side*) is a *conditional expression* which defines the result. The symbols if, then and else are reserved words. The Pascal conditional statement chooses between alternative *actions*, but the Hope conditional expression chooses between alternative *values*. This is consistent with the view that a function application is a way of writing a value rather than a recipe for computing it. If the value of the expression x > y is true, the value of the whole conditional expression is the value of x, otherwise it is the value of y. The alternative values can be defined by any Hope expressions.

When the value of a function is defined by more than one expression as they are here, the expressions are evaluated in an unspecified order. A suitable computer, such as the Imperial College ALICE machine, described in Chapter Eight, can evaluate both expressions and the test in parallel and throw away one of the values according to the result of the test.

CONSTRUCTING PROGRAMS FROM FUNCTIONS

A Hope program is just a single expression containing one or more function applications composed together. It is evaluated immediately and the result and its type are displayed on the screen. In the following example of a program using max, the output is shown in *italics*:

```
max ( 10, 20 ) + max ( 1, max ( 2,3 ) ) ;
23 : num
```

The rules for evaluating the expression are the same as those of Pascal: function arguments are evaluated first, the functions are applied, and finally other operations are performed in the usual order of priority.

Existing functions may be used to define new ones. The Hope version of MaxOfThree might look like this:

```
dec MaxOfThree : num # num # num -> num ;
--- MaxOfThree ( x, y, z ) <= max ( x, max ( y, z ) ) ;
```

A MORE INTERESTING EXAMPLE—REPETITION

Just as the Pascal conditional statement is replaced in Hope by the conditional value, so the repetitive statement is replaced by the *repetitive value*. Consider the following Pascal function to multiply two numbers using repeated addition:

```
function mult ( x, y : INTEGER ) : INTEGER ;

var prod  : INTEGER ;

begin
prod := 0 ;

    while y > 0 do
    begin
    prod := prod + x ;
    y := y - 1
    end ;

mult := prod
end ;
```

It is hard to be sure this function does enough additions (it took three tries to get it right) and this seems to be a general problem with loops in programs. A common way of checking imperative programs is to simulate their execution. For input values of 2 and 3, prod starts with the value 0 and takes values of 2, 4 and 6 on successive loop iterations, which suggests that the definition is correct. Hope has no loop construct, and all the additions which the Pascal program performed must be written in a single expression.

```
dec mult : num # num -> num ;
--- mult ( x, y ) <= 0 + x + x +  ...
```

It would be straightforward to see that this expression specified the correct number of additions, if we knew how many + x terms to write. The hand simulation suggests that y of them are needed, but the value of y is not known when the expression is written. However, for any given value of y, the two expressions:

```
mult ( x, y )      and      mult ( x, y - 1 ) + x
```

will have the same number of + x terms if written out in full. The second one always has two terms whatever the value of y, and can be used as the definition of mult:

```
--- mult ( x, y ) <= mult ( x, y - 1 ) + x ;
```

As it stands, this is a circular definition, because mult must be applied in order to find the value of mult. Remember however, that the expression is really shorthand for 0 followed by y occurrences of + x. When y is zero, the result of mult is also zero because there are *no* + x terms. In this case mult is not defined in terms of itself, so if a special test is added for it, the definition will terminate. A usable definition of mult is:

```
--- mult ( x, y ) <= if y = 0
                     then 0
                     else mult ( x, y - 1 ) + x ;
```

Functions which are defined using themselves like this are called *recursive*. Every Pascal program using a loop can be expressed as a recursive function in Hope. All recursive definitions need one case (called the *base case*) where the function is not defined in terms of itself, in the same way that all Pascal loops need a terminating condition.

FUNCTIONS AS OPERATIONS

Hope permits a function with two arguments like mult to be used as an infix operator. It must be assigned a priority and used as an operator everywhere including the equations which define it. The definition of mult as an infix operator looks like this:

```
infix mult : 8 ;
dec mult : num # num -> num ;
--- x mult y <= if y = 0
                then 0
                else x mult ( y - 1 ) + x ;
```

a larger number in the infix declaration indicates a higher priority. The second argument of mult is parenthesised because its priority of 8 is greater than that of the built-in subtraction operation. Most standard Hope functions are supplied as infix operators.

OTHER KINDS OF DATA

Hope provides two other primitive data types. A truval (truth value) is equivalent to a Pascal Boolean and has values true and false. We have already seen the expression x > y defining a truth value; > is a standard function whose type is num # num -> truval. Truth values may be used in conditional expressions and combined together with the standard functions and, or and not.

Single characters are of type char, with values a, b and so on. Characters are most often used as components of data structures such as character-strings.

DATA STRUCTURES

Significant programs need data structures and Hope has two standard kinds already built in. The simplest kind corresponds to a Pascal **record**: a fixed number of objects of any type may be bound together into a structure called a *tuple*. For example:

```
( 2, 3 )        and         ( 'a', true )
```

are tuples of type num # num and char # truval respectively. Tuples enable a function to define more than one value. This one defines the time of day given the number of seconds since midnight:

```
dec time24 : num -> num # num # num ;
--- time24 ( s ) <= ( s div 3600,
                      s mod 3600 div 60,
                      s mod 3600 mod 60  ) ;
```

div is the built-in integer division function and mod delivers the remainder after integer division. If we enter an application of time24 at the terminal, the result tuple and its type will be displayed on the screen in the usual way:

```
time24 ( 45756 ) ;

( 12,42,36 ) : ( num # num # num )
```

The second standard structured data type is called a *list* and has similar properties to a Pascal **file**. It is sequentially accessed and can contain any number of objects of the same type. We can write expressions which represent lists, such as:

```
[ 1, 2, 3 ]
```

which is of type list (num). There are two standard functions for defining lists. The infix operator : : (read as 'cons') defines a list in terms of a single object and list of the same type of object; thus:

```
10 :: [ 20, 30, 40 ]
```

defines the list:

```
[ 10, 20, 30, 40 ]
```

: : should not be thought of as adding 10 to the front of [20, 30, 40]. It really defines a *new* list [10, 20, 30, 40] in terms of two other objects without changing their meaning, rather in the same way that $1 + 3$ defines a new value of 4 without changing the meaning of 1 or 3.

The other standard list function is nil, which defines a list with no elements in it. Every list can be represented by an expression consisting of applications of : : and nil. An expression like:

```
[ a + 1, b - 2, c * d ]
```

is considered to be a shorthand way of writing:

```
a + 1 :: ( b - 2 :: ( c * d :: nil ) )
```

There is also a shorthand way of writing lists of characters. The following three expressions are all equivalent:

```
"cat", [ 'c', 'a', 't' ], 'c' :: ( 'a' :: ( 't' :: nil ) )
```

When the result of a Hope program is a list, it is always printed out in the concise bracketed notation, except for lists of characters, which are printed in quotes.

Every data type in Hope is defined by a set of primitive functions like : : and nil. They are called *constructor* functions, and are not defined by recursion equations. The definition of a tuple above actually used a standard constructor called , (read as 'comma'). Later on we shall see how constructors are defined for other types of data.

FUNCTIONS WHICH DEFINE LISTS

A Pascal program to print the first *n* natural numbers in descending order might be written as a loop which printed one value out on each iteration, for example:

```
for i := n downto 1 do write ( i ) ;
```

Since there are no loop constructs in Hope, all the values must be defined at once in a single expression, like the result of mult:

```
dec nats : num -> list ( num ) ;
--- nats ( n ) <= if n = 0 then nil
                           else n :: nats ( n-1 ) ;
```

nil is useful for writing the base case of a recursive function which defines a list. If the function is tested at the terminal by entering:

```
nats ( 10 ) ;
[ 10,9,8,7,6,5,4,3,2,1 ] : list ( num )
```

it will be seen that the numbers are in descending order. This is because they were arranged that way in the list, and *not* because they were defined in that order. The values in the expression defining the list are treated as though they were all generated at the same time. On the ALICE machine they actually *are* generated at the same time.

If the results were needed in ascending order, the final data structure would have to be constructed the opposite way round. This cannot be done by writing its definition as:

```
...  else nats ( n-1 ) :: n ;
```

because : : expects its first argument to be list component and its second to be a list. Instead, we must use another built-in operation <> (read as 'append') which concatenates two lists. The definition will then look like this:

```
--- nats ( n ) <= if n = 0 then nil
                       else nats ( n - 1 ) <> [ n ] ;
```

n is placed in brackets to make it into a (single-item) list because <> expects both its arguments to be lists. The second argument could also have been written (n :: nil) instead of [n].

DATA STRUCTURES AS PARAMETERS

Consider the definition of a function to find the sum of a list of numbers. The declaration will look like this:

```
dec sumlist : list ( num ) -> num ;
```

The right-hand sides of the equations which define sumlist will need to refer to the individual elements of the list actual parameter. This is done by using an equation whose left-hand side looks like this:

```
--- sumlist ( x :: y ) ...
```

This is an expression involving list constructors and corresponds to an actual parameter which is a list. x and y are formal parameters, but they now name *individual parts* of the actual parameter value. In an application of sumlist like:

```
sumlist ( [ 1, 2, 3 ] )
```

the actual parameter will be 'dismantled' so that x names the value 1 and y names the value [2, 3]. The complete equation will be:

```
--- sumlist ( x :: y ) <= x + sumlist ( y ) ;
```

The base case of the function will be the empty list, but it cannot be tested for directly in the equation because there is no formal parameter which refers to the whole list. In fact, the application:

```
sumlist ( nil )
```

will result in an error, because `nil` cannot be dismantled to find the values of x and y. This case must be covered separately using a second recursion equation:

```
--- sumlist ( nil ) <= 0 ;
```

The two equations can be given in either order. When `sumlist` is applied, the actual parameter is examined to see which constructor function was used to define it. If the actual parameter is a non-empty list, the first equation is used, because non-empty lists are defined using the : : constructor. The first number in the first is named x and the remaining list y. If the actual parameter is the empty list, the second equation is used because empty lists are defined using the constructor `nil`.

PATTERN-MATCHING

An expression composed of constructors appearing on the left-hand side of a recursion equation is called a *pattern*. Selecting the right recursion equation and dismantling the actual parameter to name its parts is called *pattern-matching*. A function definition must contain a recursion equation for each possible constructor defining the argument type.

Sometimes it is not necessary to dismantle the actual parameter, and the corresponding formal parameter can match the whole object, irrespective of the constructors which define it. As an example, we will define a function to concatenate two lists like the built-in operation <>:

```
infix cat : 4 ;
dec cat : list( num ) # list( num ) -> list ( num ) ;
--- ( h :: t ) cat l <= h :: ( t cat l ) ;
---           nil cat l <= l ;
```

The first list parameter is matched by the pattern(h : : t)so that its first item (the 'head') and the remaining list (the 'tail') can be referred to separately on the right-hand side. The second recursion equation covers the case when the first list is empty. The second list parameter is matched by the pattern l whether it is empty or not.

As well as writing enough recursion equations to satisfy all the parameter constructors, care must be taken not to write sets of equations in which more than one pattern might match the actual parameters, because that would be ambiguous.

We can write patterns to match arguments which are tuples in the same way using the tuple constructor ,. In the application mult (x, y)the parentheses and the comma are not part of the syntax of the application as they are in Pascal, but specify the construction of a tuple; the parentheses are only needed because , has a low priority. Hope regards all functions as having a single argument, which may be a tuple when the effect of several arguments is required. Without parentheses, the expression:

```
mult x, y
```

would be interpreted as:

```
( mult ( x ), y )
```

A recursion equation with the left-hand side:

```
--- mult ( x, y ) <= ...
```

is simply a pattern-match on a tuple. The first item in the tuple is named x and the second one y.

Pattern-matching may also be performed on num parameters. These are defined by two constructors called succ and 0. succ defines a number in terms of the next lower one. 0 has no arguments and defines the value zero. Although 0 is conventionally regarded as a *value*, we are already used to thinking of function applications as equivalent to values, so it is quite consistent to think of 0 as a function of no arguments. The following version of mult uses pattern-matching to identify the base case:

```
infix mult : 8 ;
dec mult : num # num -> num ;
--- x mult 0          <= 0 ;
--- x mult succ ( y ) <= ( x mult y ) + x ;
```

succ (y) can be read as 'the successor of some number which we will call y'. Instead of naming the actual parameter y as in the original version of mult, we are naming its predecessor.

SIMPLIFYING EXPRESSIONS

In Pascal programs complex expressions may be simplified by removing common sub-expressions and evaluating them separately. Instead of:

```
writeln ( ( x + y ) * ( x + y ) ) ;
```

most programmers would probably write:

```
z := x + y ; writeln ( z * z ) ;
```

which is clearer and more efficient. Hope programs consist only of expressions and it is even more important to simplify them. This can be done by using a *qualified expression*:

```
let z == x + y in z * z ;
```

This is *not* an assignment although it looks like one. == is read as 'is defined as' and z is local to the expression following the in. An expression such as:

```
let z == z + 1 in z * z ;
```

actually introduces a *new* z which is used in the sub-expression z * z and which hides the original one in the sub-expression z + 1. There is a second form of qualified expression which enables names to be used before their meanings are defined. It looks like this:

```
z * z where z == x + y ;
```

This defines the same result as the expression using `let`. `x + y` is evaluated first, and its value is used in the qualified sub-expression.

When the qualifying expression is a function application delivering a data structure, we can use a pattern on the left-hand side of the `==` symbol to name its components if required:

```
dec time12 : num -> num # num ;
--- time12 ( s ) <= ( if h > 12 then h-12 else h, m )
                      where ( h, m, s ) == time24 ( s ) ;
```

This construction is used most often in recursive functions which define tuples. For example, suppose we want to convert a sentence into a list of its component words. For simplicity a word is taken to be any sequence of characters, separated in the sentence by any number of blanks. The sentence and a single word will be of type `list ( char )` and the final sequence of words a `list ( list ( char ) )`. It is fairly straightforward to define a function which delivers the first word of the sentence:

```
dec firsttry : list ( char ) -> list ( char ) ;
--- firsttry ( nil )    <= nil ;
--- firsttry ( c :: s ) <= if c = ' '
                              then nil
                              else c :: firsttry ( s ) ;
```

A powerful feature of Hope is the ability to enter and display any kind of value at the terminal, making it easy to test the individual functions of a program separately. Executing `firsttry` gives:

```
firsttry ( "You may hunt it with forks and Hope" ) ;

"You" : list ( char )
```

However, this does not quite solve the problem, because we also need access to the rest of the sentence to find the remaining words. The function must deliver the remaining list of characters as well as the first word. This is where tuples must be used:

```
dec firstword : list ( char ) ->
                  list ( char ) # list ( char ) ;
--- firstword ( nil )    <= ( nil, nil ) ;
--- firstword ( c :: s )
        <= if c = ' '
              then ( nil, s )
              else ( ( c :: w, r )
                    where ( w, r ) == firstword ( s ) ) ;
```

The qualified expression is parenthesised so that it only applies to the expression after the else, otherwise firstword will be evaluated recursively as long as the sentence is non-empty, even if it starts with a blank. A typical application of firstword might appear as follows:

```
firstword ( "Hope springs eternal ..." ) ;


( "Hope", "springs eternal ..." )
: ( list ( char ) # list ( char ) )
```

firstword can be used to define the required function to split a sentence into a list of its individual words:

```
dec wordlist : list ( char ) -> list ( list ( char ) ) ;
--- wordlist ( nil )     <= nil ;
--- wordlist ( c :: s )
     <= if c = ' '
          then wordlist( s )
          else ( w :: wordlist ( r )
                where ( w, r ) == firstword ( c :: s ) ) ;
```

a trial application at the terminal might appear as follows:

```
wordlist ( "While there's life there's Hope" ) ;

[ "While", "there's", "life", "there's", "Hope" ]
: list ( list ( char ) )
```

REVIEW

So far we have concentrated on features of Hope which have something in common with traditional languages such as Pascal, but without many of their limitations, such as fixed-size data structures. We have also been introduced to the functional style of programming in which programs are no longer recipes for action, but simply definitions of data objects.

We will now examine features of Hope which lift it onto a much higher level of expressive power, and allow us to write programs which are not only extremely powerful and concise, but which can be checked for correctness at compile-time and mechanically transformed into more efficient versions (see chapter eight).

MAKING FUNCTIONS MORE POWERFUL

The Hope compiler can spot many common kinds of error by checking the types of all objects in expressions. Although this is harder than checking at run-time, it allows more efficient programs and reduces the possibility of a critical production program failing in circumstances which were not encountered in testing.

However, strict type-checking can be inconvenient when the operations performed on a data structure do not depend on the value of the data items contained in it. This can be seen clearly in Pascal when trying to write a procedure to reverse an array of *either* 10 integers *or* 10 characters.

Hope avoids this kind of restriction by allowing a function to operate on more than one type of object. We have already seen that the standard constructors : : and nil will define a list (num), a list (char) and a list (list (char)). The standard equality function = will compare any two objects of the same type. Functions with this property are called *polymorphic*. The Pascal built-in functions abs and sqr and operations like > and = are polymorphic in a primitive kind of way.

We can define our own polymorphic functions in Hope. The function cat defined above will concatenate lists of numbers, but could be used for lists containing any type of object. This is done by first declaring a kind of 'universal type' called a *type variable*. This is used in the declaration of cat where it stands for any actual type:

```
typevar alpha ;
infix cat : 8 ;
dec cat : list ( alpha ) # list ( alpha ) -> list ( alpha ) ;
```

This says that cat has two parameters which are lists and defines a list, but makes no statement about the kind of object in the lists. However, alpha always stands for the same type throughout a given declaration, so all the lists must contain the *same* type of object. The expressions:

```
[ 1,2,3 ]   cat   [ 4,5,6 ]      and         "123"   cat   "456"
```

are correctly-typed applications of cat and define a list (num) and a list (char) respectively, while the expression:

```
[ 1,2,3 ]   cat   "456"
```

is not because alpha may not be interpreted as two *different* types. The interpretation of a type variable is local to a declaration so it can have different interpretations in other declarations without confusion.

Of course it only makes sense for a function to be polymorphic as long as the equations defining it make no assumptions about types. In the case of cat the definition uses only : : and nil, which are polymorphic themselves. However, a function like sumlist uses + and can only take parameters which are lists of numbers.

USER-DEFINED DATA TYPES

Tuples and lists are quite powerful, but for more sophisticated applications, we will need to define our own types. User-defined types make programs clearer and help the type-checker to help the programmer. A new data type is introduced by means of a *data declaration*:

```
data vague == yes ++ no ++ maybe ;
```

data is a reserved word and vague is the name of the new type. == is read as 'is defined as' and ++ as 'or'. yes, no and maybe are the names for the constructor functions of the new type. We can now write function definitions which use these constructors in patterns:

```
dec evade : vague -> vague ;
--- evade ( yes )    <= maybe ;
--- evade ( maybe ) <= no ;
--- evade ( no )     <= yes ;
```

The constructors can be parameterised with any type of object, including the type which is being defined. We can define types whose objects are of unlimited size (like lists) using this kind of recursive definition. As an example, consider a user-defined binary tree which can contain numbers as its leaves:

```
data tree == empty ++ tip ( num ) ++ node ( tree # tree ) ;
```

There are three constructors: empty has no parameters and defines a tree with nothing in it. tip defines a tree in terms of a single num, and node defines a tree in terms of two other trees. We might visualise a typical binary tree like this:

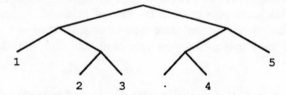

The following example of a function which manipulates trees delivers the sum of all the numbers contained in one:

```
dec sumtree : tree -> num ;
--- sumtree ( empty )         <= 0 ;
--- sumtree ( tip ( n ) )     <= n ;
--- sumtree ( node ( l, r ) ) <= sumtree ( l ) +
                                 sumtree ( r ) ;
```

Unfortunately there is no shorthand for writing tree constants as there is for list constants, so they must be written in full using constructors. To add up all the numbers in the example tree above using sumtree we must type in the expression:

```
sumtree ( node ( node ( tip  ( 1 ),
                        node ( tip ( 2 ),
                               tip ( 3 ) ) ),
                 node ( node ( empty,
                               tip ( 4 ) ),
                        tip ( 5 ) ) ) ) ;
```

This is not really a drawback, because programs which manipulate complex data structures like trees will generally define them using other functions. However, it is very useful to be able to type any kind of constant data

structure at the terminal to test an individual function like sumtree. To test
a Pascal program piecemeal, it is usually necessary to write elaborate test
harnesses or stubs to generate test data.

MAKING DATA MORE ABSTRACT

The identifier list is not really a Hope data type, but a *type constructor*
and must be parameterised with an actual type before it represents one. We
did this every time we declared a list (num)or a list (char).
The parameter can also be a user-defined type, as with a list (tree)
or even a type variable as in list (alpha), which defines a *polymorphic
data type*. Constructing new data types like this is a compile-time operation
and should not be confused with constructing new data *values* which is a
run-time operation.

We can define our own polymorphic data types, such as this version of the
earlier binary tree which can have any type of value in its leaves:

```
data tree ( alpha ) ==
     empty ++ tip ( alpha ) ++
     node ( tree ( alpha ) # tree ( alpha ) ) ;
```

Once again, alpha is taken to be the same type throughout one instance of
a tree. If it is a num, then all references to tree (alpha)are taken
as references to tree (num).

We can define polymorphic functions which operate on trees containing
any type of object, because tree constructors are now polymorphic. The
following function 'flattens' a binary tree into a list of the same type of object:

```
dec flatten : tree ( alpha )  -> list ( alpha ) ;
--- flatten ( empty )            <= nil ;
--- flatten ( tip ( x ) )        <= x :: nil ;
--- flatten ( node ( x, y ) ) <= flatten ( x ) <>
                                  flatten ( y ) ;
```

In the following examples, flatten is demonstrated on various kinds of
tree:

```
flatten( node ( tip ( 1 ), node ( tip ( 2 ), tip ( 3 ) ) ) ) ;

[ 1, 2, 3 ] : list ( num )

flatten( node ( tip  ( one ),
                node ( tip ( two ),
                       tip ( three ) ) ) ) ;

[ one, two, three ] : list ( list ( char ) )
```

```
flatten( node ( tip  ( tip ( 'a' ) ),
               node ( tip ( empty ),
                     tip ( node ( tip ( 'c' ),
                                  empty ) ) ) ) ) ;

[ tip ( 'a' ), empty, node ( tip ( 'c' ), empty ) ]
: list ( tree ( char ) )
```

Notice how the type-checker may need to go through several levels of data types to deduce the type of the result.

EVEN MORE CONCISE PROGRAMS

Polymorphic types and functions permit shorter, clearer programs. In Pascal, procedures allow the same code to operate on different data values of a specified type but polymorphic functions are much more powerful, because they can be used when data structures are the same 'shape' whatever the type of value contained in them. The same Hope function can reverse a list of numbers or characters, where two almost-identical Pascal routines would be needed to reverse an array of integers and an array of characters.

Not all operations on data structures are independent of the values contained in them. A common requirement is to apply some function to each of the primitive data items in the structure. Consider the following function to define a list (num) whose elements are the squares of another list (num) using a second function square:

```
dec square : num -> num ;
--- square ( n ) <= n * n ;

dec squarelist : list ( num ) -> list ( num ) ;
--- squarelist ( nil )      <= nil ;
--- squarelist ( n :: l ) <= square ( n ) ::
                                squarelist ( l ) ;
```

Every time we write a function which processes every element of a list, it will be almost identical to squarelist. For instance, to generate a list of factorials from a list of numbers:

```
dec fact : num -> num ;
--- fact ( 0 )            <= 1 ;
--- fact ( succ ( n ) ) <= succ ( n ) * fact ( n ) ;

dec factlist : list ( num ) -> list ( num ) ;
--- factlist ( nil )      <= nil ;
--- factlist ( n :: l ) <= fact ( n ) :: factlist ( l ) ;
```

factlist has exactly the same 'shape' as squarelist, it just applies fact instead of square and then applies itself recursively. Values which differ between applications are usually supplied as actual parameters and functions should be no exception. Hope treats functions as data objects and we can do this in a perfectly natural way. A function which can take another function as an actual parameter is called a *higher-order function*. When it is declared we must give the type of formal parameter standing for the function is the usual way. The declaration of fact tells us that its type is:

```
num -> num
```

This is read as 'a function mapping numbers to numbers'. This idea can be used to write factlist and squarelist as a single higher-order function. The new function needs two parameters, the original list, and the function which is applied inside it. Its declaration will be:

```
dec alllist : list ( num ) # ( num -> num ) -> list ( num ) ;
```

The 'shape' of alllist will be the same as factlist and squarelist, but the function applied to each element of the list will be the formal parameter f :

```
--- alllist ( nil, f )    <= nil ;
--- alllist ( n :: l, f ) <= f ( n ) :: alllist ( l, f ) ;
```

We use alllist like this:

```
alllist ( [ 2,4,6 ], square ) ;

[ 4,16,36 ] : list ( num )

alllist ( [ 2,4,6 ], fact ) ;

[ 2,24,720 ] : list ( num )
```

Notice that there is no argument list after square or fact in the application of alllist, so this construction will not be confused with functional composition. fact (3) represents a function application, but fact by itself represents the unevaluated function.

Higher-order functions can also be polymorphic. This idea can be used to define a more powerful version of alllist which applies an arbitrary function to every element of a list of objects of arbitrary type. This function is usually known as map:

```
typevar alpha, beta ;
dec map : list ( alpha ) # ( alpha -> beta ) ->
          list ( beta ) ;
--- map ( nil, f )    <= nil ;
--- map ( n :: l, f ) <= f ( n ) :: map ( l, f ) ;
```

The definition now uses two type variables alpha and beta. Each one represents the same actual type throughout one instance of map, but the two types can be different. This means that any function which maps an alpha to a beta can be used to generate a list of beta from any list of alpha.

The actual types are not restricted to scalars, which makes map rather more powerful than it appears at first sight. Suppose we have a suitable polymorphic function to find the length of a list:

```
typevar gamma ;
dec length : list ( gamma ) -> num ;
--- length ( nil )     <= 0 ;
--- length ( n :: l ) <= 1 + length ( l ) ;


length ( [ 2,4,6,8 ] ) + length ( "cat" ) ;

7 : num
```

map might be used to apply length to every element of a list of words defined by wordlist:

```
map ( wordlist ( "... the function never dies" ), length ) ;

[ 1,3,8,5,4 ] : list ( num ) ;
```

In this example alpha is taken to be a list (char) and beta to be a num, so we can deduce that the type of the function must be (list (char) -> num). length formal fits the bill if gamma is taken to be a character.

COMMON PATTERNS OF RECURSION

map is powerful because it sums up a pattern of recursion which occurs frequently in Hope programs. Another common pattern of recursion can be seen in the function length used above. Here is another example of the same pattern:

```
dec sum : list ( num ) -> num ;
--- sum ( nil )     <= 0 ;
--- sum ( n :: l ) <= n + sum ( l ) ;
```

The underlying pattern consists of processing each element in the list and accumulating a *single* value which forms the result. In sum, each element contributes its value to the final result. In length the contribution is always 1 irrespective of the type or value of the element, but the pattern is identical. Functions which display this pattern are of type:

```
( list ( alpha ) -> beta )
```

In the function definition, the equation for a non-empty list parameter will specify an operation whose result is a beta. This is + in the case of length and sum. One argument of the operation will be a list element and the other will be defined by a recursive call, so the type of the operation needs to be:

```
( alpha # beta -> beta )
```

This operation differs between applications, so it will be supplied as a parameter. Finally a parameter of type beta is needed to specify the base case result. The final function is usually known as reduce. In the following

definition, the symbol ! introduces a Hope comment, which finishes with
another ! or with a newline:

```
dec reduce : list ( alpha ) #              ! original list
             ( alpha # beta -> beta ) # ! reduction operation
             beta ->                       ! base case value
             beta ;                        ! result type
--- reduce ( nil, f, b )     <= b ;
--- reduce ( n :: l, f, b ) <= f ( n, reduce ( l, f, b ) ) ;
```

To use reduce as a replacement for sum the standard function + must be
supplied as an actual parameter. To do this it must be prefixed by the symbol
nonop to tell the compiler not to treat it as an infix operator:

```
reduce ( [ 1,2,3 ], nonop +, 0 ) ;

6 : num
```

When reduce is used to implement length, the first argument of the
reduction operation is irrelevant because we always add 1 whatever the list
element is. This function ignores its first argument:

```
dec addone : alpha # num -> num ;
--- addone ( _ , n ) <= n + 1 ;
```

_ can be used to represent any formal parameter which is not referred to on
the right-hand side of the equation:

```
reduce ( "a map they could all understand", addone, 0 ) ;

31 : num
```

Like map, reduce is much more powerful than it first appears because the
reduction function need not define a scalar. Consider the following function
which inserts an object into an ordered list of the same kind of object:

```
dec insert : alpha # list ( alpha ) -> list ( alpha ) ;
--- insert ( i, nil )     <= i :: nil ;
--- insert ( i, h :: t ) <= if i < h
                            then i :: ( h :: t )
                            else h :: insert ( i, t ) ;
```

Actually this is not strictly polymorphic as its declaration suggests, because
it uses the built-in function <, which is only defined over numbers and
characters, but it shows the kind of thing that can be done. Using insert
to reduce a list of characters has the effect of sorting them:

```
reduce ( "All sorts and conditions of men", insert, nil ) ;

"    Aacddefiillmnnnnoooorsssstt" : list ( char )
```

The sorting method (insertion sort) is not very efficient, but the example
shows something of the power of higher-order functions and of reduce in

particular. Later we shall see that it is even possible to define map in terms of reduce.

Of course map and reduce only work on list (alpha) and we must provide separate versions for each of our own structured data types. This is the recommended style of Hope programming, because it makes programs largely independent of the 'shape' of the data structures they use. As an example, consider an alternative kind of binary tree which holds data at its nodes rather than its tips, and a reduce function for it:

```
data tree ( alpha ) ==
    empty ++
    node ( tree ( alpha ) # alpha # tree ( alpha ) ) ;

dec redtree : tree ( alpha ) #
              ( alpha # beta -> beta ) #
              beta -> beta ;
--- redtree ( empty, f, b )
    <= b ;
--- redtree ( node ( l, v, r ), f, b )
    <= redtree ( l, f, f ( v, redtree ( r, f, b ) ) ) ;
```

This kind of tree can be used to define a more efficient sort. An *ordered* binary tree has the property that all the objects in its left subtree logically precede the node object, and all those in its right subtree are equal to the node object or logically succeed it. To build an ordered tree we need a function to insert new objects into an already-ordered tree, such as:

```
dec instree : alpha # tree ( alpha ) -> tree ( alpha ) ;
--- instree ( i, empty ) <= node ( empty, i, empty ) ;
--- instree ( i, node ( l, v, r ) )
    <= if i < v
       then node ( instree ( i, l ), v, r )
       else node ( l, v, instree ( i, r ) ) ;
```

A list can be sorted by inserting its elements successively into an ordered tree using instree, then flattening the tree back into a list. This is very easy to specify using the two kinds of reduction defined above:

```
dec sort : list ( alpha ) -> list ( alpha ) ;
--- sort ( l ) <= redtree( reduce ( l, instree, empty ),
                           nonop ::, nil ) ;

sort ( "Mad dogs and Englishmen" ) ;
"   EMaadddegghilmnnnoss" : list ( char )
```

ANONYMOUS FUNCTIONS

When using map and reduce, it was necessary to define extra functions like fact and square to pass in as parameters. This is inconvenient when they are not needed anywhere else in the program and especially when they are trivial, like `sum` or `addone`. For immediate use in cases like this, we can define an anonymous function called a *lambda-expression*. The following lambda-expression corresponds to `sum`:

```
lambda ( x, y ) => x + y
```

The symbol `lambda` introduces the function and `x` and `y` are its formal parameters. The expression `x + y` is the function definition. The part after `lambda` is just a recursion equation without the `---` and with `=>` instead of `<=`. Here is another lambda-expression used as the actual parameter of `reduce`:

```
reduce ( [ "toe", "tac", "tic" ],
         lambda ( a, b ) => b <> a, nil ) ;

"tictactoe" : list ( char )
```

The lambda-expression may be defined by more than one recursion equation. They are separated from each other by the symbol | and the appropriate one is selected by pattern-matching in the usual way. In the following example, a second equation is used in the lambda-expression to avoid division by zero when the function it defines is executed:

```
map ( [ 1,0,2,0,3 ],
      lambda ( 0 )             => 0
          | ( succ ( n ) ) => 100 div succ ( n ) ) ;

[ 100,0,50,0,33 ] : list ( num )
```

Finally, as promised above, here is the definition of `map` using `reduce`.

```
dec map : list ( alpha ) # ( alpha -> beta ) ->
          list ( beta ) ;
--- map ( l, f )
    <= reduce( l, lambda ( n, b ) => f ( n ) :: b, nil ) ;
```

FUNCTIONS WHICH CREATE NEW FUNCTIONS

Hope functions possess 'full rights': not only can they be passed as actual parameters like any data object, but a function can also be delivered as the *result* of another function. The result can be a named function or an anonymous function defined by a lambda-expression, for example:

```
dec makestep : num -> ( num -> num ) ;
--- makestep ( i ) <= lambda ( x ) => i + x ;

makestep ( 3 ) ;

lambda ( x ) => 3 + x : num -> num
```

A test evaluation of makestep shows that its result is indeed a lambda-expression which adds a fixed quantity to its single argument. The size of the increment was specified as an actual parameter to makestep when the new function was created, and has become 'bound in' to its definition. The new function may itself be evaluated as follows:

```
makestep ( 3 ) ( 10 ) ;

13 : num
```

There are *two* applications here. First makestep is applied to 3, then the resulting function is applied to 10. Finally, here is an example of a function which has a function both as its actual parameter and as its result:

```
dec twice : ( alpha -> alpha ) -> ( alpha -> alpha ) ;
--- twice ( f ) <= lambda ( x ) => f ( f ( x ) ) ;
```

twice defines a new function which has a single argument and some other function f bound into its defintion. The new function has the same type as f. Its effect can be demonstrated using the function square:

```
twice ( square ) ;

lambda ( x ) => square( square ( x ) ) : num -> num

twice ( square ) ( 3 ) ;

81 : num
```

The new function applies the bound-in function to its argument twice. It is even possible to bind in twice itself, generating a new function which behaves like twice except that the function eventually bound in will be applied *four* times:

```
twice ( twice ) ;

lambda ( x ) => twice ( twice ( x ) )
: ( alpha -> alpha ) -> ( alpha -> alpha )

twice ( twice ) ( square ) ( 3 ) ;

43046721 : num
```

CONCLUSION

In this chapter some of the ideas of 'functional programming' have been introduced through one of the new generation of functional languages. A Hope program consists of a series of functions regarded as definitions of data structures. The 'results' of the program are specified by a single expression, and the powerful idea of higher-order functions allows common program patterns to be captured in a single function.

Some of these ideas will already be familiar to users of LISP, but they appear in a purer form in Hope, because there are no mechanisms for updating data structures like the SETQ and RPLACA of LISP or for specifying the order of evaluation like GO and PROG.

We have also seen features which are primitive or absent from LISP and from most imperative languages. Complex data types may be defined without specifying their representation using the data declaration and pattern-matching used to decompose them. In this way abstract data types may be used directly without writing access procedures and without the need to invent superfluous identifiers. The typing mechanism allows the compiler to check that data objects are used in a correct and consistent way, while the idea of polymorphic types stops the checking from being too restrictive and enables common data 'shapes' to be defined by a single function. Higher-order functions and polymorphic types permit very concise programs. Programmers are more productive because programs are easier to understand and reason about.

3

An Introduction to FP and the FP Style Of Programming

Peter Harrison and Hessam Khoshnevisan

INTRODUCTION

In 1978, John Backus introduced a functional style of programming in which variable-free programs are built from a set of primitive programs by a small set of combining forms (functionals) which are also often referred to as 'program forming operations' (PFOs) and by recursive definitions. This style is embodied in the language FP, which facilitates the manipulation of the functions themselves, rather than repeatedly creating new objects from old ones in some auxiliary domain. FP thus relates to a higher level of analysis than do the more common, object-oriented functional languages. In fact, FP has its own functional algebra which prescribes rules for the manipulation of functions and so simplifies reasoning about programs.

In passing, it may be noticed that the comparison of FP with other functional languages such as Hope, may be viewed as analogous to the comparisons which have been made between APL and conventional imperative languages such as Pascal. APL has a powerful set of primitive functions and operators, which can be used to solve quite significant problems in a very small number of statements (or even just a few symbols) without requiring any loops. The main criticisms made of APL have been its very terse syntax and structure. However, after becoming familiar with the new notation, its critics tend to reduce their objections to two: multiple assignment to a single variable and the use of computed, typeless goto statements. Both of these are, of course, absent from functional languages including FP.

In this chapter we first consider the constituents of an FP system before giving some examples to illustrate the style of programming that FP encourages. The final section outlines the motivation behind the definition of FP and compares the FP style of functional programming with the programming style of languages such as Hope or Miranda. We point out that FP emphasizes operations on programs and algebraic properties which facilitate reasoning at a higher level of generality. (A consequence of this is that program transformation becomes simplified as we discuss in more detail in Chapter Six).

FP SYSTEMS

An FP system consists of the following:-

1. A set of *primitive* functions (for example the arithmetic operators +,-,*, etc).

2. A set of program forming operations, or 'PFOs'. These are programming constructs analogous to while loops, conditionals and so on, found in conventional languages like Pascal, and they may be used to create more complex functions from simpler ones.

3. A domain of objects which might be, for example, integers, characters, sequences, etc.

User defined functions are defined in terms of these FP system components.

PFOs are the programming constructs of FP (like 'while', 'if then else', etc., of Pascal), and differ from the programming constructs of other languages (including other functional languages) in that they are predefined operations on *functions* as opposed to *objects*. We are all familiar with the conditional statements, such as (if P then Q else R) statements in Pascal. The conditional operation of FP (f → g ; h) is similar except that the predicate, and the true and false branches of the conditional, are expressions involving *only* functions, namely f, g and h. These expressions can be primitive functions, user-defined functions or expressions built using the PFOs. All PFOs take a number of functions as their arguments and return a single FP function as their result. FP functions take a single object as their input and produce a single object as their result, ie. they are of type (object → object). All FP systems are equipped with an operation called 'application', which, given a function and an object, produces the result of applying the function to the object. The notation f : x is used to represent the application of function f to the object x.

To define a particular FP system we must specify the set of primitive functions, the set of PFOs, and the set of objects. Listed below are some examples of primitives which might be present in an FP system. They are the only PFO's that will be used in the program examples that follow. The meaning of each is given by specifying the result of its application to various kinds of objects. If they are applied to any other kind of object not mentioned in their meaning, the result of the application will be ⊥. (⊥ is pronounced 'bottom' and denotes the undefined object or error). So, for example, an attempt to add the integer 1 to the character a will yield ⊥ since a is not of the correct type for the + primitive.

TABLE 1:   SOME POSSIBLE PRIMITIVES

Add, Subtract, Multiply, Equals, etc $(+, -, *, \text{eq}, \text{etc})$

When x is of form $<y, z>$ and y,z are numbers then $+:x$ yields the sum of y and z otherwise $+:x = \perp$ (The others are defined similarly)

Greater Than, Less Than or Equal, etc $(\text{gt}, \text{le}, \text{etc})$

When $x=<y, z>$ & y,z are numbers then if $y>z$ then $\text{gt}:x = T$ else $\text{gt}:x = F.$
(The others are defined similarly)

And, Or, Not $(\text{and}, \text{or}, \text{not})$

When $x=<T, T>$ then $\text{and}:x = T$

When $x=<F, T>$ or $x=<T, F>$ or $x=<F, F>$ then $\text{and}:x = F$
(or is defined similarly)

When $x=T$ then $\text{not}:x = F$

When $x=F$ then $\text{not}:x = T$

Null (null)

When $x= <>$ then $\text{null}:x = T$

When $x = <x_1, \ldots, x_n>$, $n \geq i$ then $\text{null}:x = F$

Otherwise $\text{null}:x = \perp$

Append Left (al)

when $x=<y, <>>$ then $\text{al}:x = <y>$

When $x= <y, <z_1, \ldots, z_m>>$ then $\text{al}:x = <y, z_1, \ldots, z_m>$

Append Right (ar)

When $x=<<>, y>$ then $\text{ar}:x = <y>$

When $x= <<z_1, \ldots, z_m>, y>$ then $\text{ar}:x = <z_1, \ldots, z_m, y>$

Selectors $(1, 2, 3, \ldots)$

suppose $x=<z_1, \ldots, z_m>$. If $m \geq i$ then z_i
else $\perp$

Right Selectors $(1r, 2r, 3r, \ldots)$

As above, selects first, second etc from the right of the sequence.

Identity $\text{id}:x$

$\text{id}:x = x, \forall x$

x *Transpose* (trans)

When x= $<<>, \ldots, <>>$ then trans:x = $<>$

When x= $<x_1, \ldots, x_m>$ where $x_i = <x_{ii}, \ldots, x_{kk}>$
  for $1 \leq i \leq m$
then trans:x = $<z_1, \ldots, z_k>$ where
$z_j = <x_{ij}, \ldots, x_{mj}>$ for $1 \leq j \leq k$
otherwise trans:x = $\perp$

Distribute Left (distl)

When x=$<y, <>>$ then distl:x =$<>$

When x=$<y, <z_1, \ldots z_m>>$
  then distl:x = $< <y, z_1>, \ldots, <y, z_m> >$

Distribute Right (distr)

When x=$<<>, y>$ then distr:x =$<>$

When x=$< <z_1, \ldots z_m>, y>$
  then distr:x = $< <z_1, y>, \ldots, <z_m, y> >$

Iota (iota)

If $x = 0$ iota:x = $<>$
then if x is a positive integer iota:x = $<1, 2, \ldots, x>$
otherwise iota:x = $\perp$

Others

Some other possible primitives are, head (hd), tail (tl), right tail (tlr), rotate left (rotl), rotate right (rotr), subtract one (sub1), is-equal-to-zero (eq0), and so on. Note that all these can just as easily be written in FP using the primitives and the PFOs. For example,

```
def eq0 = eq∘[id, 0̄]
def sub1 = -∘[id, 1̄]
```

Listed below are some examples of the type of PFOs that could be chosen for an FP system.

TABLE 2: SOME POSSIBLE PRIMITIVES

Composition
$$(f \circ g):x = f:(g:x)$$
Construction
$$[f_1, f_2, \ldots, f_m] : x = < f_1:x, f_2:x, \ldots, f_m:x >$$
Condition
$$(p \to f; g) : x = \text{if } (p:x) \text{ is T then } f:x$$
$$\text{else if } (p:x) \text{ is F then } g:x$$
$$\text{else } \perp$$

Insert Left

$$/f \; : \; x \; = \quad \text{if } x = <y> \text{ then } y$$
$$\text{else if } x = <y_1, \; \ldots, \; y_m> \; \& \quad m{\geq}2$$
$$\text{then } f:<y_1, \; /f:<y_2, \ldots, y_m>>$$
$$\text{otherwise } \bot$$

Insert Right

$$\backslash f \; : \; x \; = \quad \text{if } x = <y> \text{ then } y$$
$$\text{else if } x = <y_1, \; \ldots, \; y_m> \; \& \quad m{\geq}2$$
$$\text{then } f:<f:\backslash f:<y_2, \ldots, y_{m-1}>, \; y_m>$$
$$\text{otherwise } \bot$$

Apply to All

$$\alpha f \; : \; x \; = \; \text{if } x = <> \text{ then } <>$$
$$\text{if } x = <y_1, \; \ldots, \; y_m> \text{then } <f:y_1, \; \ldots \; , f:y_m>$$

Constant

$$\overline{f} \; : \; x \; = \; \text{if } x = \bot \text{ then } \bot$$
$$\text{otherwise } k$$
$$\text{(NB. here f is an object parameter)}$$

The set of objects is determined by the set of atoms chosen. For example if we choose to consider the set of integers, the set of non-empty strings, and the atoms T and F denoting true and false then

        T, 66, -88,   0, c, Hello, F,   GHj

all are valid atoms.

Considering now the set of objects which we can write down, we have that:-

1. Every atom itself is an object.

2. All sequences of objects, denoted by $<x_1, x_2, \ldots x_m>$ $m \geq 0$ (where each x_i is an object excluding, $\bot$, $1 \leq i \leq n$), are also all objects.

3. $\bot$ is also an object.

Some examples of objects we can obtain from the atoms defined above are:-

        Hello, $\bot$, -98, <66, T, ac>, <>,

        < <>, <JF>, H, <jj, <0>, u>, c> and so on.

User Defined Functions

The set of primitives and PFOs determines the set of functions which can be defined by the user. These are defined using the **def** statement in FP. For example,

        def MyFunction =   +

defines MyFunction to be equal to the primitive FP function +,

    def MyFunction = MyFun2

defines MyFunction to be equal to another user-defined function i.e. to MyFun2,

    def MyFun =   AFun → BFun; CFun

defines a function in terms of an FP PFO—in this case the conditional. Note that as already mentioned, AFun, BFun, and CFun must all be functions (which can themselves be built by the use of other PFOs).

Each PFO takes a number of functions as parameters. The number of parameters is determined by the particular PFO. The 'conditional' PFO takes 3 parameters, whereas the 'construction' PFO can accept any number of function parameters. Recursive function definitions are allowed, so in the above example any of the expressions AFun, BFun, or CFun can refer to MyFun.

Note that the syntax for function application and composition in basic FP can be rather clumsy, for example

    add:<2,3> as opposed to 2+3,

    al:<2, <3,4,5> > as opposed to 2::<3,4,5>

However, it is easy to incorporate infix notation into many variable free functional expressions. We can, for example, define *infix* functions :: and + where

    f::g represents al∘[f, g]

    f+g represents +∘[f, g]

but note that if f = [h, g], the expression +∘f is clearer than (1∘f) + (2∘f) or (1+2)∘f.

So, to summarise what we have said so far:- An FP system comprises a set of primitive functions or operations, a set of predefined PFOs and a domain of objects, to the elements of which we can apply functions. Given such a system, we can build more complex functions (user defined functions) which are expressed in terms of the components of the FP system, and these functions can refer to themselves. When a function is applied to an object the application yields a result which is another object. Objects may be either atoms, the special undefined object ⊥, or sequences, each element of which is itself a valid, i.e. non-bottom, object.

In the next section, we describe how programs may be written in FP and the style of programming that FP encourages.

PROGRAMMING IN FP

A user defined function is defined by one and only one definition. The name given to the function must be unique and must not coincide with a name

associated with the primitive functions or PFOs. No part of a definition is a
result itself; instead each part is a function that must be applied to an
argument to obtain a result.

Here are four simple examples of user defined functions:-

```
def last = null∘tl → 1; last∘tl
def len  = null → 0 ; +∘[1̄, len∘tl]
def cat  = null∘1 → 2; al∘[1∘1, cat∘[tl∘1, 2] ]
def fact = eq0 → 1̄; *∘[id, fact∘sub1]
```

The first returns the last element of a sequence; the second returns the length
of a sequence; the third catenates two sequences, and the last defines the
well-known factorial function.

Taking the factorial example given above, some of the intermediate
expressions that an FP implementation would obtain in evaluating fact:2
are:-

```
    fact:2

=>  (eq0 → 1̄ ; *∘[id, fact∘sub1]):2

=>  *∘[id, fact∘sub1]:2          (because eq0:2 = F)

=>  *∘[id:2, fact∘sub1:2]

=>  *:<2, fact:1>

=>  *:<2, *:<1, fact:0> >        (because eq0:0 = T)

=>  *:<2, *:<1, 1̄:0> >

=>  *:<2, *:<1, 1> >

=>  *:<2, 1>

=>  2
```

Observe that the examples of function definitions given above, although
written in FP, are written in a recursive style which is familiar from
conventional functional languages such as Hope, LISP or Miranda. For
instance, the definition of last says that if the tail of the sequence is empty
then select the first element of the object; otherwise look for the last element
of the tail of the object using a recursive call to last. In the FP style it is
often possible to replace an explicitly recursive definition by an equivalent
non-recursive functional expression.

The function last could, in most systems, be expressed purely in terms
of primitives. For example

```
def  last = 1r
```

Similarly a more natural FP definition for factorial is

> **def** f = (/*)∘iota

(This 'inserts' a * between each element of the sequence <1,2,...,n>).
A function to catenate ('append' in Hope) two sequences is

> **def** cat = (/al)∘ar

This non-recursive definition successively appends an item from the end of
the first sequence on to the beginning of the second. Note that /cat will
then be a function that concatenates any number of sequences.

The function len, for length, in some systems might be a primitive, but
if not, the more natural FP definition could be

> **def** len = null → $\bar{0}$; /+∘(α$\bar{1}$)

This definition says that len:x is 0 if x is empty; otherwise it is given by
changing each element of x into a 1, and then adding up the 1s. The items
are literally counted!

Observe that the more 'natural' FP solutions are non-recursive (effectively
the recursion has been 'pushed' into the PFOs used). Although these non-
recursive definitions may look strange initially, they express an equally
obvious solution. By becoming familiar with the high level PFOs, and their
concise syntax, it is possible to give concise, expressive, and flexible definitions
which are often non-recursive, using just a few symbols. (It has been suggested
that programmer productivity is inversely proportional to the number of
characters required in a program!) Here, then, are some more complex
examples:-

Example 1, Vector Product

We can define the function VectorProduct to be

> **def** VP = (/+)∘(α*)∘trans

Application of VP to a pair of equal length vectors first creates the sequence
of matched pairs of components (result of trans), then multiplies each
pair, and finally sums these results. For nonequal length vectors, the result
of trans is ⊥ and so therefore is the result of VP. We can explain each
step in evaluating VectorProduct applied to the pair of vectors < <1,2,3>,
<6,5,4> > as follows:

> VP   : < <1,2,3> , <6,5,4> >

By def of VP	=>	(/+)∘(α*)∘trans:<<1,2,3>,<6,5,4>>
Effect of composition	=>	/+:(α*:(trans:<<1,2,3>,<6,5,4>>)
Applying Transpose	=>	/+:(α*:<<1,6>,<2,5>,<3,4>>)
Effect of ApplyToAl	=>	/+:<*:<1,6>,*:<2,5>,*:<3,4>>
Applying *	=>	/+:<6,10,12>

Effect of Insert   => +:<6, +:<10,12>>

Applying   => +:<6,22>

Applying again   => 28

Example 2, Matrix Multiply

We can define the function MatrixMultiply (MM) to yield the product of any pair $<y,z>$ of conformable matrices, where each matrix is represented as the sequence of its rows:

```
y = < y₁, ..., yₖ>
        where  yᵢ = <yᵢ₁, ..., yᵢₗ> for i = 1,...,k
        1,k ≥ 1

z = < z₁, ..., z₁>
        where  zᵢ = <zᵢ₁, ..., zᵢₘ> for i = 1,...,l
        m ≥ 1
```

def MM = (ααVP)∘(αdistl)∘distr∘[1,trans∘2]

The program has four steps: Reading from right to left, each is applied in turn, beginning with [1,trans∘2]. If the argument is the pair of matrices $<y,z>$ the first step yields $<y,w>$ where w is the transpose of z. The second step yields $<<y_1,w>,...,<y_k,w>>$, where the y_i are the rows of y. The third step yields $<distl:<y_1,w>,...,distl:<y_k,w>>$ = $<p_1,...,p_k>$ where $p_i=<<y_i,w_1>,...,<y_i,w_k>>$ for i=1,...,k and w_j is the jth column of z (jth row of w) for j= 1, ..., l Thus p_i is a sequence of row and column pairs. ααVP, causes αVP to be applied to each p_i, which in turn causes VP to be applied to each row and column pair in each p_i. The result of the last step is thus the sequence of rows comprising the product matrix. If either matrix is not rectangular, or if the length of a row of y differs from that of the column of z, or if any element of y or z is not a number, the result is ⊥, produced by trans or VP.

Example 3, Binary Tree Insert

Suppose that a binary tree is represented by a sequence of three elements, where the first element is the left binary tree, the second is the data at the node (which we shall assume is a number) and the third is the right binary tree. A function Insert which inserts a number into a tree in such a way that all elements in the left subtree of any node are less than the smallest number in the whole of the right subtree of the same node, might look like this:-

```
def Insert = null∘1 → [ [], 2, [] ];

    le∘[2∘1, 2] → [ 1∘1, 2∘1, Insert∘[3∘1, 2] ];

    [ Insert∘[1∘1, 2], 2∘1, 3∘1 ];
```

Example 4, Part Product

A function ParProds, which, when given a sequence of integers $\langle x_1, \ldots, x_m \rangle$, produces a sequence of integers $\langle y_1, \ldots, y_m \rangle$ such that for each i, $1 \leq i \leq m$ $y_i = x_1 * \ldots * x_i$

> Thus ParProds∘iota : 5 = <1,2,6,24,120>
> i.e. the sequence of factorials of the numbers 1 to 5.
> We may start from the observation that ParProds : $\langle x_1, \ldots, x_m, y \rangle$
>
> = PARar : < ParProds:$\langle x_1, \ldots x_m \rangle$, y>
>
> where PARar = ar∘[1, *∘[1r∘1, 2]]

Unfortunately, we can not simply replace the recursive call to ParProds by a right-insert of the PARar function, because it requires that the sequence to which it is applied has a sequence for its first element. We first have to make this element into a sequence. The function ParProds therefore becomes

> **def** ParProds = null → $\overline{0}$; (\PAR ar)∘al∘[[1], tl]
>
> **def** PARar   = ar∘[1, *∘[1r∘1, 2]]

We may now use this (non-recursive) function in the definition of other useful functions.

Example 5, Polynomial Evaluation

Consider the problem of producing the function, EvalPoly, to evaluate a polynomial when applied to the pair consisting of the sequence of the polynomial's coefficients and the value of its variable. For example, suppose the variable is denoted by x whose value is 6, then

> EvalPoly : <<3,1,4,2>,6> = $3 + x + 4x^{**}2 + 2x^{**}3$
>   = 585

An approach to programming this function is to generate a sequence comprising the powers of the x value, and then to multiply each element of this sequence with the corresponding element of the coefficient sequence, and then to sum the resulting sequence i.e.:-

> **def** EvalPoly = VP∘[1, PolyPowers]
> (where VP is the vector product already defined)

To define the PolyPowers function, we can generate a sequence of copies of x which has the same length as the sequence of coefficients, and then apply our ParProds function to that sequence. In the above case, this would give

> PolyPowers : <<3,1,4,2>,6> = ParProds : <6,6,6,6>

In fact, this is not quite correct because x to the power of 0 is 1, so the first coefficient (that for x to the power of 0) needs to be multiplied by 1. This is accomplished by having `PolyPowers` append a 1 to the start of the sequence produced by `ParProds`, which now has length equal to one less than the number of coefficients:

```
def PolyPowers = al°[1̄, ParProds°GenXSeq]
def GenXSeq    = nCopy∘[sub1∘length∘1, 2]
```

Now all that is required is the function nCopy, which, given a pair $\langle n, x \rangle$, produces a sequence of n copies of x. Perhaps the most obvious way to do this is via a recursive function:-

```
def nCopy  = eq1∘1 → tl ; al∘[2, nCopy∘[sub1∘1, 2]]
```

However, by using iota purely as a counter, a non-recursive definition can be obtained;

```
def nCopy = (α1)∘distl∘[2, iota∘1]
```

Bringing these functions together, we get

```
def EvalPoly    = VP∘[1, PolyPowers]

def PolyPowers  = al°[1̄, ParProds°GenXSeq]

def GenXSeq     = nCopy∘[sub1∘length∘1, 2]

def nCopy       = eq1∘1 → tl ; al∘[2, nCopy∘[sub1∘1, 2]]
```

Note that in our hierarchically structured solution to this problem, we have defined auxiliary functions which may be equally useful in other problems. Note that nCopy and VP are general functions which will work on any sequences of the correct shape. With a little modification PolyPowers could be made more general so that when applied to a sequence $\langle n, x \rangle$, will produce a sequence comprising the first n powers of x.

COMPARISION WITH THE HOPE STYLE

FP's main objectives are to provide a higher level, more structured functional system that is easier to model mathematically than others at present available. It attempts to achieve these objectives via

1. object abstraction
2. higher level function-forming operations
3. restrictions on function-forming operations

We now consider these in turn and see what each implies.

Object Abstraction

FP is based on the notion that it is practicable to use a programming language almost entirely free of variables; programs would be defined using operations on other programs (i.e. functions). These operations are given in terms of FP's Program Forming Operations. Hence FP emphasises application of functionals to functions to produce new functions, and so in a sense, FP 'moves up a level'.

Higher Level Function Forming Operations

In the FP style the idea is that users ought not to be allowed to define their own PFOs. This restriction can be used to advantange, since languages which allow definition of new PFOs (i.e. arbitrary higher order functions) are in some sense too powerful a formalism for programming purposes. Well designed restrictions on this power will, it is claimed, lead to clearer and more structured programs.

Functional languages other than FP, have, in one sense or another, only one PFO, that of functional abstraction. In this way any required higher-order function can be user-defined, including all of the PFOs that FP may possess. The power of this facility is not in question, but the drawback is that the programmer is often encouraged, or even forced, to overspecify a solution to a problem. For example the programmer might use tail recursion to process the elements of a list which is a level of detail that may be totally unnecessary for the solution of the problem. FP with its set of high level PFOs allays this problem to a considerable extent—recall the example cat to name but one. The PFOs in many cases provide a natural solution which is non-recursive, in much the same way as the 'APL one-liners' avoid loops.

Restrictions on function forming operations

Under the FP philosophy, PFOs should have attractive algebraic properties as well as being constructs with good expressive power. The language is therefore easier to model mathematically as well as well-structured from the programming viewpoint.

A simple Algebra of functional programs is associated with an FP system which can be used by the ordinary programmer to prove his programs correct. This contrasts with the more conventional methods of correctness proving, because we do not have to map the program into some domain of discourse such as mathematical functions, or predicate transformers in order to reason about it. The language that we use to reason about the program will essentially be FP itself.

A simplified structure of programs is important if programming is to become a mathematical discipline that is useful to the programming community. The simpler the structure of programs, the more easily a programmer can recognise that part of his program contains instances of one or more theorems that will help him prove its correctness or make it more efficient.

For example, in the Hope style it is difficult to recognise an instance of a simple law like

$$[f, g]^\circ h = [f^\circ h, g^\circ h]$$

The chances of recognising instances of more significant theorems must surely be very small, yet many useful theorems do exist. Instances can often be recognised readily in FP. Similarly manipulation of programs by transformation systems (which involves recognition of instances of theorems) will become easier.

CONCLUSION

To conclude, we have seen that FP is radically different from other functional programming languages. Its main objectives are to provide a higher level, more structured functional system in which it is easier to develop solutions to problems and which is easier to model mathematically than others presently available. Much remains to be done to make it a truly practical programming language, and future work in a wide range of areas is required.

Some areas for future work include extensions such as strong typing, local definition facility and inclusion of facilities in the language to make programs more readable and a complete compile-time type checking system.

Functional Programming Using Abstract Data Types

Roger Bailey

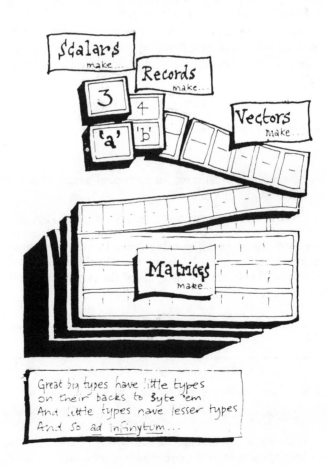

PASCAL DATA STRUCTURES

A powerful feature of modern imperative languages such as Pascal is the
way in which 'simple' data objects such as integers and characters can be
grouped together into larger objects or data *structures*. For example we can
group a fixed number of integers into a one-dimensional **array**, or an integer
and a character into a **record** and so on. Data structures can be formed into
more elaborate ones, for instance records can be grouped into one-dimensional
arrays and one-dimensional arrays into two-dimensional ones. Writing a
program to solve a problem is often mainly a matter of choosing an appropriate
structure to represent the data.

However, the data-structuring facilities of Pascal are not quite as powerful
as we might like and often *restrict* the way we write programs because the
built-in structures do not always have suitable properties for the problem we
are trying to solve. When we require a structure with properties which the
language does not supply, we will *simulate* it using the built-in types. We do
this so often that we probably think it is a strength of Pascal when it is really
a weakness that we need to do it at all.

For example, consider how we would use Pascal if it only allowed one-
dimensional arrays with lower bounds of one. When we needed arrays with
different lower bounds, we would *simulate* them. In 'real' Pascal we can
declare:

```
var Vec : array [ a..b ] of SomeType ;
```

and refer to an element as:

```
Vec [ i ]
```

In 'cut-down' Pascal a one-dimensional array with the same number of
elements might be declared as:

```
var Sim : array [ n ] of SomeType ;
```

where n would have the value b−a+1. (This assumes that we would not
need to state the lower bound in 'cut-down' Pascal, since it is always 1.) The
relationship between the elements of the two arrays for the case where Vec
has bounds of [−2..3] is as follows:

Vec [−2]	Vec [−1]	Vec [0]	Vec [1]	Vec [2]	Vec [3]
Sim [1]	Sim [2]	Sim [3]	Sim [4]	Sim [5]	Sim [6]

The element of Sim corresponding to Vec [i] is:

```
Sim [ i−a+1 ]
```

This may be just acceptable, but rapidly becomes intolerable when we have
to simulate arrays with more than one dimension:

```
var Tab : array [ a..b, c..d ] of SomeType ;
```

The equivalent one-dimensional array which simulates `Tab` will contain $(b-a+1)*(d-c+1)$ elements. The relationship between the two arrays for the case when `Tab` has dimensions [0..2, 4..5] is:

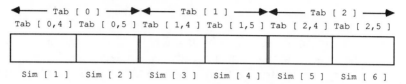

The element of `Sim` which corresponds to `Tab` [i,j] is:

```
Sim [ (i-a)*(d-c+1)+j-c+1 ]
```

It is far from obvious that this expression refers to the same element as the 'real' Pascal expression.

The real reason data-structures are useful in Pascal is *not* because they are flexible, but because they provide a clear notation for writing programs. If the notation exactly fits the problem they assist the programmer, but if they must be used to simulate some other structure, the notation impedes understanding and it becomes very easy to make careless clerical errors.

A MORE INTERESTING DATA STRUCTURE

We will now consider a data structure which is needed in many practical programming problems and which Pascal does not supply directly. A *binary tree* is a structure containing three components. The first is some piece of data which we want to store and retrieve. This may be a simple item like an integer or a character, or something more complex such as a record or a character-string. The other two components are themselves binary trees, called the left and right *subtrees*. We can visualise part of a binary tree as follows:

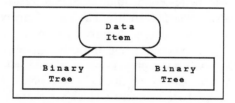

Everything in a *rectangular* box is abinary tree

This definition is not very useful for actually constructing a binary tree because it is *recursive*; binary trees are defined in terms of themselves. Before we can construct one, we first require two others. We escape from the recursive definition by allowing a second kind of binary tree which does not contain another tree. In fact it contains *no* items at all. It looks like this:

```
Empty
```

This kind of tree cannot be used for storing data, but only for terminating the branches of trees which already contain data. Here is a picture of a finite binary tree constructed from a mixture of the two kinds of subtree:

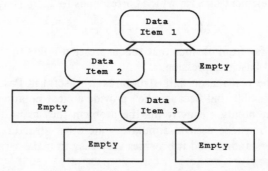

Each of the boxes (either Empty or Data) is called a *node*.
The top node of the tree is called the *root*.

When reasoning about trees, it is helpful to visualise them as two-dimensional objects like the examples in the diagrams. It is hard to retain this simple view in an actual program which uses binary trees because they must be simulated using Pascal data objects such as records and pointers. We can reason about the pictorial trees using abstract operations such as 'take the left subtree', but the same operation on the simulated tree must be written as an expression involving pointers. To generate a new node it is necessary to write several lines of code to create a new record using NEW and initialise its fields correctly. The logic of any program which manipulates binary trees soon becomes obscured by pointer assignments and calls to NEW and DISPOSE; understanding and debugging become extremely difficult.

However, with some preparatory work and self-discipline, the simple view of binary trees can be retained. First a small set of high-level operations (such as 'take the left subtree') which are characteristic of trees is identified. When an appropriate Pascal data structure has been chosen to represent binary trees, each of the high-level operations is implemented as a separate Pascal procedure called an *access procedure*. All operations on binary trees must now be performed using only the access procedures, which will be the only parts of the program which refer to real Pascal data structures. In this way, the binary tree becomes a well-defined type of data object with a small number of operations upon it just like the built-in data types of Pascal. It is called an *abstract data type*.

The following set of six access procedures defines the binary tree abstract data type. For the time being we will only consider their *properties*; we will say nothing about the type of data stored in a node nor anything about the way binary trees are represented. The first two access procedures are for building new binary trees and are called *constructor* functions:

> EmptyTree   This takes no arguments and returns an empty binary tree, that is, one containing no data items.
>
> ConsTree   This takes a data item and two binary trees as arguments and returns a *new* binary tree whose root is the same as the data item and whose subtrees are the same as the two binary trees.

Three access procedures are required to refer to the three component parts of a binary tree. These are called *selector* functions and each one takes a single binary tree as its argument:

> ValOf   This returns the data item at the root of the argument.
>
> LeftTree   This returns the left subtree of the argument.
>
> RightTree   This returns the right subtree of the argument.

It is an error to use any of the selector functions on an empty binary tree, since it has no components. The final access procedure is a Boolean function called a *predicate* function which can be used to test for an empty binary tree.

> IsEmptyTree   This takes a single binary tree as its argument and returns TRUE if it is empty and FALSE if not.

Binary trees must *only* be referred to using these functions. This protects against accidently corrupting one by making a coding mistake in the piece of program which manipulates it. By adhering to the discipline of using only the access procedures, a further advantage is obtained. If the implementation of the abstract data type is changed, perhaps to make it run faster or use less storage, only the code of the access procedures need be changed. Provided their properties and parameters remain the same, it is not necessary to change any program which uses them.

There is one difficulty with using abstract data types in Pascal programs. Ideally the real Pascal type used to represent the abstract type should be hidden to avoid the temptation of bypassing the access procedures. In ISO Pascal, this is not possible because the access procedures must be defined within the program which uses them. In some Pascal dialects (such as Pro-Pascal and UCSD) the *code* of an access procedure can be hidden by compiling it separately and declaring it as *external* in the program which uses it. However, it is still necessary to declare the real type used to implement the abstract data type and thus to reveal its representation Pascal Plus from Queens University, Belfast is a notable exception to this. This is really a shortcoming of standard Pascal, not of abstract data types.

In standard Pascal the best we can do is to exercise self-discipline and not use any properties of the representation directly. For instance, if the abstract data type has been implemented using pointers, no pointer variable must be updated or even examined directly, even if it seems harder to use the access procedure. Later we will see an implementation of binary trees using pointers in which the empty tree is represented by the NIL pointer. It is clearly more trouble to define IsEmptyTree and write:

```
if IsEmptyTree( t )
```

than simply to write:

```
if t = NIL
```

The reason for avoiding the latter construction is that if the test for NIL were made directly in a program which used binary trees, it would not be possible to change their implementation later without changing every reference to NIL in the program. A little discipline now can save a great deal of work later on.

PROGRAMMING USING FUNCTIONS

The access procedures defining the binary tree abstract data type are all functions; furthermore there is no way of *changing* any part of a binary tree. To obtain this effect, ConsTree must be used to build a *completely new* tree using the appropriate parts of an existing binary tree and any new values which we want to introduce.

This might seem like a very inefficient way to write Pascal programs, but there is a lot of evidence to suggest that changing the values of variables is a major factor in making programs hard to understand and get correct. The logical extension of this point of view is that *no* variable should change its value. Unlikely as it seems, it turns out that not only can such a program be written, but it is even possible to write one which does not use any variables at all. The technique is to build a single data structure (such as a binary tree) containing all the required 'results' of the program, which is then written as a function returning this structure as its result.

As an example, suppose there exists an implementation of binary trees which can contain single characters at their nodes. An efficient program can be written for sorting characters by constructing an *ordered binary tree*. This has the property that, for any given character at a node, all the characters in the left subtree precede it in the alphabet, and all those in the right subtree are equal to it or follow it. When such a tree has been built, it is only necessary to remove (or print), the characters in the correct order to get the effect of sorting them.

As it is not immediately obvious how to write a function which constructs an ordered tree of characters, we will consider the easier problem of inserting a single character into the correct position in an existing ordered tree. This is done by comparing the new character with the character at the root of the tree. If the new character precedes the root character alphabetically, it belongs in the left subtree, otherwise in the right. The operation is then repeated on the appropriate subtree until the end of a branch is reached and the new character added at that point.

Here is a Pascal function to insert a character into an ordered binary tree of characters, or more accurately, to construct a *new* ordered tree containing all the original characters and the new one in its correct position.

```
function Insert ( c : CHAR ; t : TREE ) : TREE ;
begin
if IsEmptyTree ( t )

    then { Return a TREE containing only "c" }

    Insert := ConsTree ( c , EmptyTree , EmptyTree )

    else
    if c < ValOf ( t )

        then {  "c" belongs in the left subtree of "t", so return a new TREE whose
               root and right subtree are the same as "t", and whose left
               subtree is formed by inserting "c" into the old left subtree of
               "t". }

        Insert := ConsTree ( ValOf ( t ) ,
                             Insert ( c , LeftTree ( t ) ) ,
                             RightTree ( t ) )

        else {  "c" belongs in the right subtree of "t". This time the new tree
               has the same root and left subtree as "t", but its right subtree
               is the result of inserting "c" into the old right subtree of "t".
               }

        Insert := ConsTree ( ValOf ( t ) ,
                             LeftTree ( t ) ,
                             Insert( c , RightTree ( t ) ) )

    end ;
```

When reading the function definition, remember that its arguments will be evaluated *before* the function itself. This is one way in which we can specify the order of evaluation when we program with functions. We do not change any part of the binary tree, but always generate a new one containing the original values and with the new character in its correct position.

If the new character cannot be added directly to the end of a branch, it must be inserted into one of the subtrees. This is the same problem as the one we are already trying to solve, except that the tree we are using is smaller. The problem is thus defined recursively, and a recursive program is a natural way of expressing its solution.

The new character gets added to the end of a branch when the succession of smaller subtrees eventually ends with an empty tree. Instead of using a

loop to express the idea of examining successive subtrees until we reach the
end of a branch, we use recursion to express the idea of forming a new subtree
by inserting the character into the old one. It is easy to convince ourselves
that the function is correct, because no values get changed anywhere. All
binary trees are newly-generated.

Insert may now be used to build an ordered tree from a sequence of
characters by starting with an empty tree and adding the characters one at
a time. To input the characters we want to sort, we will assume the existence
of a function ReadChar which returns the next character from the standard
input file and that the end of the input sequence is marked by some unique
character, perhaps a period. The following function builds an ordered binary
tree from an existing tree and a file of input characters:

```
function BuildTree ( c : CHAR ; t : TREE ) : TREE ;
begin
if c = '.'

  then  { No more characters, so return 't' as we found it }

  BuildTree := t

  else  { Repeat the operation on the next input character, but supplying as
          the argument a new TREE built with 'Insert'.  This consists of the
          nodes of 't' with 'c' now in its correct position. }

  BuildTree := BuildTree ( ReadChar , Insert ( c, t ) )

end ;
```

Once again we express repetition by recursion[1]. Before we start building the
ordered tree, all the characters are in the input file and none in the growing
binary tree, which is therefore empty. We can build the complete binary tree
from the whole input file by writing the expression:

```
BuildTree ( ReadChar , EmptyTree ) ;
```

As an example, the sequence of characters:

M E R C U R Y .

will be converted into the following tree (empty subtrees have been omitted
for clarity):

[1]   Experienced 'functional programmers' may object that *BuildTree* appears to work by
using the side-effect produced on the input file by *ReadChar*. This is not strictly necessary and
has been done to avoid the complication of introducing a second type of data structure.
BuildTree can be written without side-effects by replacing the input file with a linear list data
structure. At each step, the first character in the list must be inserted into the growing tree and
the remaining characters in the list passed to the recursive application of *BuildTree*, which
can be arranged to terminate when the list of characters is empty. This has the additional
advantage of not requiring a special character to mark the end of the input.

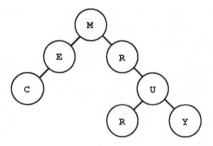

We can determine by inspection that the character at each node of the tree is later in the alphabet than any character in its left subtree, and earlier than (or equal to) any one in its right subtree; hence the characters have been sorted as they were inserted.

To see the sorted list of characters, they must be removed from the tree in the right order. The rule is that we start at the root and remove (or print) all the characters from the left subtree (because they come before the node character), then the node character itself, and finally all the characters in the left subtree (because they come after the node character). The problem of removing the characters from the subtree is the same as the main problem we are trying to solve, so just as we used recursive functions to construct the tree we will use a recursive procedure to print its components in the required order. It looks like this:

```
procedure PrintTree ( t : TREE ) ;
begin
if IsEmptyTree ( t )

    then { nothing to print, so return without action }

    else { "t" contains at least one character }
    begin
    PrintTree( LeftTree  ( t ) ) ; { print its left subtree first  }
    WRITE     ( ValOf     ( t ) ) ; { then the character at the node }
    PrintTree( RightTree ( t ) )   { and finally its right subtree }
    end

end ;
```

Notice that when a tree contains only one character, the recursive calls to print its left and right subtrees will both terminate without printing anything, because their arguments will be empty trees. This means that we never need to examine lower-level trees before trying to process them recursively.

Finally, we can assemble the three routines to give a complete program to sort a file of characters terminated by a full stop. All we need to do is to pass the ordered binary tree we built earlier to the PrintTree procedure:

```
PrintTree( BuildTree ( ReadChar , EmptyTree ) ) ;
```

The entire sort program has been written with no assignment statements and with no variables. The only thing we need to actually make it work is an implementation of the abstract data type TREE.

There are many ways to do this. Provided the access procedures have the properties we originally specified, it does not matter how they work internally; the tree-sort program will still work. Here is a set of access procedures which meets the specification (although the error-handling is rather crude). First we need the *type* definition for binary trees. This must be added to the main program which calls PrintTree.

```
TREE = ↑NODE ;


NODE =  record
            Value       : CHAR ;
            Left, Right : TREE
            end ;
```

Now for the code of the access procedures. In a standard Pascal program this will appear at the top level of the main program. In a UCSD or Pro-Pascal program it will be placed in a separate **unit** or **segment** respectively and only the **external** declarations will appear in the main program.

```
function EmptyTree : TREE ;
begin
EmptyTree := NIL
end ;


function ConsTree ( c : CHAR ; l_, r : TREE ) : TREE ;

var Temp : TREE ;

begin
NEW ( Temp ) ;

  with Temp↑ do
  begin
  Value := c ;
  Left  := l ;
  Right := r
  end ;

ConsTree := Temp
end ;


function ValOf ( t : TREE ) : CHAR ;
begin
if IsEmptyTree ( t )
  then WRITELN ( 'ERROR - can''t take ValOf empty tree' )
  else ValOf := t↑.Value
end ;
```

```
function LeftTree ( t : TREE ) : TREE ;
begin
if IsEmptyTree ( t )
 then WRITELN ( 'ERROR - can''t take LeftTree of empty TREE' )
 else LeftTree := t↑.Left
end ;


function RightTree ( t : TREE ) : TREE ;
begin
if IsEmptyTree ( t )
 then WRITELN( 'ERROR - can''t take RightTree of empty TREE' )
 else RightTree := t↑.Right
end ;


function IsEmptyTree ( t : TREE ) : BOOLEAN ;
begin
IsEmptyTree := ( t = NIL )
end ;


function ReadChar : CHAR ;
begin
ReadChar := INPUT↑;
GET ( INPUT )
end ;
```

In cases where the access procedures can be compiled separately, the following declarations will be needed in the main program:

```
function EmptyTree                          : TREE    ; external ;
function ConsTree    ( c    : CHAR ;
                       l, r : TREE  ) : TREE    ; external ;
function ValOf       ( t    : TREE  ) : CHAR    ; external ;
function LeftTree    ( t    : TREE  ) : TREE    ; external ;
function RightTree   ( t    : TREE  ) : TREE    ; external ;
function IsEmptyTree ( t    : TREE  ) : BOOLEAN ; external ;
function ReadChar                          : CHAR    ; external ;
```

For simplicity the program does not prompt for input. When it runs, just type in any sequence of characters terminated by a full stop and the output will consist of the same sequence in sorted order (including blanks).

CONCLUSION

In this chapter, we have seen how it is possible to define data types with specified restricted properties and how to hide their implementation from programs which use them. In particular we have seen how this idea may be used to implement complex data structures in such a way that they can (or appear to) be returned as the results of functions. By augmenting the power of Pascal functions in this way, it becomes possible to write a complete program using only functions (except for printing the final results) and without variables or assignment statements. Parameters are considered to be only temporary names for values supplied to functions; they are not variables and are never changed in this style of programming.

What we have seen is *not* just a clever parlour trick, but a different and liberating way to write programs. Once we get used to the idea of using functions which can return large data structures, programs become much easier to reason about. We need never ask a question like 'what value did X have the third time round the loop?' or 'what is the value of Y after procedure P has been executed?'. There *are* no loops and the answer is that X and Y retain the *same* values throughout the program. The only thing we ever do is to generate *new* values using old ones.

Of course we pay a price for this, which is that we keep on using new storage for the new values rather than re-using the old space by assigning new values to it. In languages like Hope which are specially designed for writing this style of program, storage which is no longer needed is recovered automatically when it is known to be safe, and this is not a problem. In spite of this, if you code and run the sort program, you will be surprised at how little storage it actually uses. The reason for this is hidden inside the code of ConsTree. Suppose we have two trees A and B, each consisting of 1000 data nodes. If we now write an expression like:

```
ConsTree ( 'Z' , A , B )
```

we might expect to generate a new tree containing 2001 nodes. Now look at the code of ConsTree. You will see that it creates only a single node (approximately three words of store) and copies into it the character 'Z' and the two pointers representing the trees A and B.

Trees which become incorporated into several different bigger trees are actually *shared* between all the trees which contain them. Try adding a counter to ConsTree and see for yourself how much storage the tree-sort program uses. Suppose that we change a tree which is shared; does this not mean that all the trees which share it will get changed as a side-effect? The answer is 'no' because the access procedures ensure that there is *no way of changing* any part of a tree. If we forbid assignment, we gain the freedom to share data structures and use store in the most economical way.

Part II
Tools

Software Development in Declarative Languages

John Darlington

TOWARDS A SCIENCE OF PROGRAMMING

Is programming a craft or a science? Most professional (and amateur) programmers would like to claim that what they do is scientific, but compared with the standards attained in other, more mature, engineering disciplines such as aeronautical or civil engineering, programming has a long way to go. If one were asked to build a bridge I doubt that it would be acceptable to construct an initial version, try it out and when it fell down correct the mistakes made in the design, and then repeat the process until the bridge stayed up. This is, however, the paradigm that most practicing programmers follow as they debug their program towards a working state. At present, programming suffers from a lack of notations for building models or initial specifications of systems and any criteria for judging the correctness of solutions to such specifications.

As the cost of hardware decreases the proportion of the cost of any total system attributable to software becomes larger. If it is difficult enough to develop complex software in the first place, the problems get even worse if one wishes to maintain or enhance an existing complex software system.

Advances have been made toward solving this problem. The invention of the first high level languages, such as Fortran, represented a significant advance over the use of machine code and vastly improved programmer productivity. It is a pity that not many other substantial advances have been made on the software side. Modern high level languages do not differ radically from Fortran and structured programming, the white hope of the 60s and 70s, has demonstrably failed to provide the final solution.

All these developments, from new languages to fancy editors and other utilities, seem to be of a kind that, although they will undoubtedly increase programmers' output (often of incorrect code!), seem incapable of enabling programming to make the transition from an inexact to an exact science. Our goal should be the precision of mathematics. No one feels the need to debug a mathematical theorem or rely on laws that are probably correct apart from a few residual bugs. Programs are superficially similar to mathematical notations, so why can't we share their degree of certainty?

The proponents of declarative languages claim that it is possible to make programming an exact mathematical science, with all the accompanying economic benefits, but that a necessary condition for this to happen is the abandonment of conventional languages and the adoption of declarative ones.

There is a fundamental distinction between the declarative languages and conventional (or even unconventional) procedural ones such as Pascal. Declarative languages are *referentially transparent* while procedural ones are not. Referential transparency is a property of language systems. A system is referentially transparent if the meaning of a whole can be derived solely from the meaning of its parts. All mathematical notions are referentially transparent. Thus the meaning (value) of a mathematical expression such as $(3+2) * (2+1)$ can be derived from the meaning of its components. Thus $3+2$ has value 5 and $2+1$ has value 3. Knowing these we can derive the meaning of the whole expression, 15.

A consequence of this property is that there is a simple substitutive equality relation between expressions in any referentially transparent system. Expressions that have the same meaning can be freely substituted for one another in any context without changing the meaning of the whole. Thus $3+2$ and $4+1$ have the same meaning (5) and $4+1$ can be substituted for $3+2$ in $(3+2) * (2+1)$ giving $(4+1) * (2+1)$. It is the possession of this property that makes mathematics an exact deductive science.

Laws can be developed that allow the formal (syntactic) manipulation of expressions and are guaranteed to preserve the meaning of the expressions being manipulated. The distributive law of arithmetic, $(x+y) * z = (x*z) + (y*z)$, is an example of such a law. Using this we can convert $(4+1) * (2+1)$ to $4 * (2+1) + 1 * (2+1)$ and know that the meaning is not changed. Referential opacity means that a system's behaviour may be time dependent, i.e. the meaning of a fragment may depend on the history of what happened prior to the evaluation of that fragment and that no simple, meaning preserving, deductive rules can be developed for that system.

Conventional programming languages are not referentially transparent. The presence of variables that are shared between procedures and the assignment statement means that the meaning of any conventional program is potentially time dependent and there is no simple substitution property, see Fig. 5.1.

Declarative languages are, by definition, referentially transparent. The meaning of any fragment of a declarative language program depends only on the meaning of its components and not at all on the history of any

The following program fragment illustrates how the behaviour of a Pascal program can be history sensitive.

```
var switch:boolean;
begin
        switch:=false;

        function f(n:integer) : integer;
        begin
        switch:=true;
        f:=2*n
        end;

        function g(n:integer):integer;
        begin
        if switch then g:=3*n else g:=4*n
        end;

        writeln(g(2) + f(1));
        writeln(f(1) + g(2));
    end;
```

Fig. 5.1   A referentially opaque Pascal Program.

The presence of the global variable, switch, makes the meaning of g dependent on the history of the computation performed prior to its evaluation. Thus g(2) + f(1) evaluates to 10 but f(1) + g(2) evaluates to 8. Thus the commutativity of +, one of the simplest manipulation laws viz X+Y = Y+X, does not apply in Pascal programs.

computation performed prior to the evaluation of that fragment. From this simple distinction many benefits flow.

The absence of any time dependent behaviour implies that declarative programs are easier to write and understand. Many burdens concerned with organising or comprehending the sequencing of events are removed from the programmer. Declarative languages are therefore intrinsically more powerful descriptive notations.

The absence of time dependent behaviour also means that subexpressions can be evaluated in any order and therefore in parallel leading to a whole range of new, highly parallel, machines designed specifically for declarative language. Several of these are described in Part III.

From the software development viewpoint the critical advantage referential transparency brings to the declarative languages is the ease with which formal manipulation systems can be developed for declarative programs.

The existence of such manipulation systems makes the process of program development by *program transformation* feasible in the declarative languages. The ideas behind program transformation stem from a diagnosis that many of the difficulties met in developing programs arise from trying to satisfy two, often conflicting, goals simultaneously. A program must be *correct*, that is it meets its specification and is free of bugs, and *efficient*, that is it computes the required results in reasonable time and makes minimal use of resources.

The first goal is best met by making a program as clear and obvious as possible. Meeting the second often involves sacrificing clarity for the sake of an intricate but efficient evaluation strategy. Given this diagnosis of the disease, the cure prescribed by transformation is fairly obvious. It is to develop your program in two separate stages concentrating on satisfying one goal at each stage. Thus a programmer first writes an initial version or *specification* of his program concentrating on making it as clear and as obviously correct as possible. Only when he is satisfied that he has a correct and complete initial version does he turn his attention to satisfying the requirement of efficient execution. This is achieved by successively manipulating or transforming the program into more and more efficient versions. It is crucial that the manipulations performed do not change the meaning of the program. Thus, to be successful, transformation depends on the existence of a set of manipulation rules capable of improving performance but guaranteed to preserve the meaning of a program. It is the availability of such manipulation rules that makes transformation feasible in declarative languages and very difficult in procedural ones.

Note that the initial specification is itself a program. As we shall see later, if one really puts one's mind to it, one can write such wonderfully inefficient programs that it is straining the meaning somewhat to call them executable! But that is the whole point, by maximising the clarity and obviousness of the initial version one is making, it is much more likely to be correct. It does, however, mean that the transformations have to be pretty powerful and capable of achieving improvements in performance way beyond that achievable by conventional optimising compilers. Characteristically one is looking for improvements in the order of the program's efficiency, for example, transforming algorithms that compute in exponential time to linear or logarithmic ones. As we shall see below such improvements are possible.

The design of optimising compilers for conventional languages such as Fortran or Pascal has developed to a fine art. Some of the optimisations these compilers perform, such as strength reduction or code lifting, can be expressed as source to source manipulations and are therefore strictly program transformations. However the sort of transformations we are seeking can be characterised as ones that can cause changes of *nature* not just changes of *degree*. Only in rare, pathological, cases are optimising compilers capable of producing as output a program totally different from their input; we need to be able to do this routinely.

The second consequence of having specifications which are executable as programs is that they can be exercised and tested against the informal requirements or modified to meet changing requirements. Thus a process of rapid prototyping is possible.

A SIMPLE TRANSFORMATION

Let us now look at a transformation. The example we have chosen to start with is fairly trivial and will not require large improvements in efficiency;

nevertheless it will serve to introduce the transformations used and illustrate that simple manipulations can produce significantly altered programs.

Say we have been asked to find the average of a list of numbers. The textbook definition of average is the sum of all the numbers divided by how many of them there are. If we take this as the basis for our obviously correct initial program, in Hope we get something of the form

```
dec average, sum, count:list (num) -> num;
```

```
---    average(l)  <=  sum(l)  div count(l);                    (1)

---    sum(nil)  <=  0;                                         (2)

---    sum(n::l)  <=  n+sum(l);                                 (3)

---    count(nil)  <=  0;                                       (4)

---    count(n::l)  <=  1 + count(l);                           (5)
```

This program is clearly correct but on a sequential machine involves the slight inefficiency that the list is traversed twice. Any self respecting Pascal programmer would collect both the sum and the count on one pass over the list.

Let us derive such a program in Hope by systematic manipulation of the original one. We shall present the transformations in an informal manner. Each step will take a program, a set of equations, and produce new equations. Informally we hope that it will be obvious that all the new equations are consequences of the existing equations and thus cannot change the meaning of the program as a whole. Formally all our transformations will use rules from the unfold/fold transformation system. See Fig. 5.2.

The first step in our transformation is to introduce a definition for a new function, av.

```
dec av:list (num) -> num x num;
```

```
---    av(l)  <=  (sum(l),  count(l));                          (6)
```

For correctness purposes the only thing we have to concern ourselves with is that introducing this new definition cannot change the meaning of our program. Since av is not mentioned at all in the previous equations this is clearly true. Quite why we introduced this particular definition is another question. The situation is analogous to the use of constructions in geometry. Introducing the right construction enables proofs to be carried out but can never enable anything false to be proved. Quite where the idea for the right construction comes from in the first place is more mysterious.

The formal reading of an equation such as

```
---    av(l)  <=  (sum(l),  count(l));
```

is that the expression on the left hand side, av(l) is equal to the expression

The unfold/fold system consists simply of six rules that allow new equations to be introduced that are consequences of existing equations.

(i) *Definition.* Introduce a new recursion equation whose left hand expression is not an instance of the left hand expression of any previous equation.

(ii) *Instantiation.* Introduce a substitution instance of an existing equation.

(iii) *Unfolding.* If $E <= E'$ and $F <= F'$ are equations and there is some occurrence in F' of an instance of E, replace it by the corresponding instance of E' obtaining F'', then add the equation $F <= F''$.

(iv) *Folding.* If $E <= E'$ and $F <= F'$ are equations and there is some occurrence in F' of an instance of E', replace it by the corresponding instance of E obtaining F'', then add the equation $F <= F''$.

(v) *Abstraction.* We may introduce a where clause, by deriving from a previous equation $E <= E'$ a new equation

```
E<=E' [u1/F1,...,un/Fn]
      where (u1,...,un) == (F1,...,Fn)
```

(E[E1/E2] means E with all occurrences of subexpressions E2 replaced by E1.)

(vi) *Laws.* We may transform an equation by using on its right hand expression any laws we have about the primitives (associativity, commutativity, etc.) obtaining a new equation.

Fig. 5.2   The unfold/fold transformation system.

on the right hand side, (sum(l), count(l)), for all values of l. If the equation is true for all l it is true for some particular *instance* of l. Thus we can *instantiate* this equation by setting l to nil getting the equation

```
    ---    av(nil)  <=  (sum(nil),  count(nil));              (7)
```

(7) is obviously a consequence of (6) so cannot alter its meaning. But (2) and (4) give values for sum(nil) and count(nil) allowing us to deduce that

```
    ---    av(nil)  <=  (0, 0);                               (8)
```

which as well as being true about av begins to look like part of a program for av.

Returning to (5) and this time instantiating l to x::l we get

```
    ---    av(x::l)  <=  (sum(x::l),  count(x::l));           (9)
```

(3) and (5) allow us to deduce

```
    ---    av(x::l)  <=  (x+sum(l),  1+count(l));            (10)
```

But we can re-arrange this using the Hope *where* construct to

```
---    av(x::l)  <=  (x+u,  1+v)
                 where  (u,v)  ==  (sum(l),  count(l));  (11)
```

Now we see that `(sum(l), count(l))` appears as the right hand side. But this is the right hand side of (6). Thus, it is equal to the left hand side of (6), `av(l)`. Because of referential transparency the `<=` can be read as `=`. Thus we can replace `(sum(l), count(l))` by `av(l)` getting

```
---    av(x::l)  <=  (x+u,  1+v)
                 where  (u,  v)  ==  av(l);           (12)
```

(8) and (12) now constitute an efficient program for `av` but do not at the moment help us with `average`. Returning to (1)

```
---    average(l)  <=  sum(l)  div  count(l);
```

we get

```
---    average(l)  <=  u div v
                 where(u,v)  ==  (sum(l),  count(l));
```

and thus

```
---    average(l)  <=  u div v
                 where  (u,  v)  ==  av(l);
```

Collecting the useful equations together we get a new program for average

```
dec  average:list(num)->  num;
dec  av:list(num)->  num  x  num;

---    average(l)  <=  u div v
                 where  (u,  v)  ==  av(l);

---    av(nil)  <=  (0,  0);
---    av(x::l)  <=  (x+u,  1+u)
                 where  (u,  v)  ==  av(l);
```

This final program, we would claim, is not so obviously correct as our initial version but is more efficient in that only one pass is performed over the list. The crucial point is that there is no need to conduct a separate proof to show that our final program is equivalent to the initial one, it is correct by construction. Neither do we have to conduct proofs to show the intermediate steps are legitimate, the correct application of the rules can be checked syntactically (and therefore mechanically).

The above example illustrated the tranformation techniques but only achieved a moderate increase in performance. To give credence to our claim that transformation can achieve substantial performance increases let us quickly look at a classic transformation, the conversion of the exponential definition of the fibonnaci function to a linear version i.e. converting a definition that takes 2^n steps to compute `fib(n)` to one that takes n steps.

Initial Program

```
dec fib:num -> num;

---   fib(0) <= 1;
---   fib(1) <= 1;
---   fib(succ(succ(n))) <= fib(n+1) + fib(n);
```

Transformation

```
dec g:num -> num x num;
---   g(n) <= (fib(n+1), fib(n));
```
                                                        Definition

```
---   g(0) <= (fib(1), fib(0));
```
                                                        Instantiation
```
        <= (1, 1);
```
                                                        Unfold

```
--- ` g(succ(n)) <= (fib(n+2), fib(n+1));
```
                                                        Instantiation

```
            <= (fib(n+1) + fib(n), fib(n+1));
```
                                                        Unfold
```
        <= (u+v, u)
            where (u, v) == (fib(n+1), fib(n));
```
                                                        Abstract
```
        <= (u+v, u)
            where (u, v) == g(n) ;
```
                                                        Fold

```
---   fib(succ(succ(n)))
            <= u+v
            where (u, v) == (fib(n+1), fib(n));
```
                                                        Abstract
```
        <= u+v
            where (u, v) == g(n);
```
                                                        Fold

Final Program

```
dec fib:num -> num;
dec g:num -> (num x num)

---   fib(0) <= 1;
---   fib(1) <= 1;
---   fib(succ(succ(n))) <= u + v
                                where (u,v) == g(n);
---   g(o) <= (1, 1);
---   g(succ(n)) <= (u+v, u)
                        where (u, v) == g(n);
```

Here the improvement in performance is much greater but the similarity
between this and the previous transformation is appealing. Our pulling the
correct definitions out of a hat may be slightly offputting but their origin is

not quite as mysterious as it seems. They can be systematically derived by investigating the pattern of computation of the specification program and identifying repeated, and therefore unnecessary, computations.

PRACTICALITY AND USEFULNESS OF TRANSFORMATION

If we are proposing, as we are, that transformation can bring about a revolution in software development and lift programming onto a new plateau of scientific rigour, we must evaluate its potential very severely. To be ultimately useful any transformation methodology must satisfy three criteria. First of all it must be correct, that is meaning preserving. Secondly it must be adequate or complete, so that all desired program developments can be achieved using the methodology; and finally it must be expressive enough so that, not only can all developments be expressed, but they can be done so in an intelligible and communicable manner. Let us see how functional languages and the unfold/fold methodology being proposed here meet these criteria.

CORRECTNESS AND COMPLETENESS

It is of course crucial that any system used for transformation preserves meaning. This property has been shown to hold for the unfold/fold system. There is one thing that has to be watched out for in doing transformations, however. It is possible using the unfold/fold system to produce a program that will fail to terminate the input values for which the original specification program will terminate! Happily there are simple guidelines that ensure that the system can be used without fear of introducing non-termination. See Fig. 5.3.

COMPLETENESS

The other question that needs to be asked of any transformation system is, how adequate or complete is it? Can any transformation that you would like to achieve be expressed using only rules from the system? The answer for the unfold/fold system is in theory no but in practice yes. There are some pathological examples of pairs of (functional) programs that are demonstrably equivalent but which cannot be transformed one to the other without stepping outside the strict confines of the system. A simple example of this is contained in Fig. 5.3. However, much work based on the unfold/fold system has demonstrated its practicality and wide range of applicability. In the years since its introduction, the unfold/fold system and related systems have been much studied and have formed the basis for many case studies.

The repertoire of the types of transformational operations that can be expressed using the unfold/fold system is quite impressive. It includes

(i) Loop Combinations. The essence of the *average* example was that there were two independent loops that needed to be combined for efficiency. Many transformations are instances of this type of transformation.

(ii) Recursion Removal. Using transformation it is possible to convert fully recursive definitions such as

```
dec fact:num -> num;
---   fact(0) <= 1;
---   fact(succ(n)) <= (n+1) * fact(n);
```

(i) Non-termination can be introduced.

Consider the very simple Hope program

```
dec f:num -> num;
---  f(n) <= 3;
```

If we fold this with itself we get

```
--- f(n) <= f(n);
```

which is undoubtedly a true fact about `f` but not a very useful method of computing values for `f` !

Generally there is a danger of producing a non-terminating program from one that terminates if the transformation used contains more fold steps than unfold steps. Thus to be safe we need to keep a count of the different steps used during a transformation. Alternatively we can check that the final program still terminates, which is impossible to do generally but often very simple in practice.

(ii) Some transformations are not possible.

Consider the functions f1 and f2

```
dec f1:num -> num'
--- f1(0) <= 0;
--- f1(succ(n)) <= 1+f1(n);

dec f2: num -> num;
---   f2(n) <= n;
```

`f1` and `f2` are obviously equivalent and `f2` can be transformed to `f1` but `f1` cannot be transformed to `f2` which is the direction we would like to go. The problem is that `f2` has no recursion at all on the right hand side so cannot be produced using a fold step. To derive `f2` we would have to guess its definition and then prove equivalence. Happily, realistically sized programs rarely have this problem.

Fig. 5.3 Correctness and completeness of the unfold/fold system.

to linear forms such as

```
dec fact:num -> num;
dec factit:num x num -> num;
---   fact(n) <= factit(n, 1);
---   factit(0, acc) <= acc;
---   factit(succ(n), acc) <= factit(n, (n+1) * acc);
```

The important point about the latter definition is that it can be executed without using a run time stack and can be simply converted to a program using only a *while* loop in a language such as Pascal. The early work on transformation viewed the functional program as an initial specification and aimed at a program in an imperative language as the final output. With the development of efficient implementations for functional languages and the imminent arrival of specially designed parallel machines, this aspect of the transformation work has tended to become less important.

(iii) Abstract Data Types. One of the more impressive applications of the basic transformation methodology has been the work on the systematic derivation of implementations for abstract data types. In order to support an abstract data type, for example trees or priority queues, in an imperative language such as Pascal, one has to write a lot of code providing implementations for the access functions of the abstract type in terms of the primitives of the concrete types provided in the language. This often results in an inefficient final program and one that is cumbersome and difficult to maintain or move to other implementation bases. Work based on functional languages and transformation has shown how efficient implementations can be automatically synthesised from a specification of the abstract and concrete types and a single mapping function formalising how the concrete type is to be used to represent the abstract one.

(iv) Program Synthesis. As we shall see below, in a functional language, we are able to write specifications that define a program more by properties it must satisfy rather than a computational recipe, however inefficient, for its evaluation. Such specifications can also be converted to efficient programs but we should perhaps talk more of program *synthesis* rather than program *transformation*. The crucial point is that both specification and program are still expressed using the same notation and there is no discontinuity between forms that are specifications and forms that are programs.

(v) Transformation for Parallel Evaluation. Early work on transformation concentrated on producing programs that would run efficiently on conventional sequential machines. For a parallel machine different program forms are needed for efficient execution. Happily exactly the same transformation methodology enables us to produce these forms as enables us to produce efficient sequential ones.

Amongst the significant transformational developments studied by transformation workers are sorting algorithms, compilers, parsing algorithms, text formatters, editors, operating systems and numerical algorithm libraries. Particular academic interest has been shown in analysing the relationships between different algorithms for a particular task, such as sorting, by systematically synthesising all the algorithms in the class from a common very high level specification. Studies of algorithms for sorting, parsing and searching have exposed pleasing symmetries and relationships between algorithms previously considered unrelated.

It would be misleading to give the impression that work has reached the stage whereby any program development, however large or complex, can be easily expressed using transformation, and even more misleading to imply that the whole process is about to be mechanised and programmers are about to become redundant. What we would claim is that transformation offers one the possibility that programming can progress from an art to a science and that even this possibility is precluded if one continues with the conventional languages. Furthermore sufficient progress is being made on extending the practicality of transformation techniques particularly in the area of partial mechanisation that we can feel optimistic about the future.

EXPRESSIBILITY AND USEABILITY

The final parameter governing transformation's ultimate usefulness is how expressive can we be using transformation? It is no point having a wonderfully formal system if any significant transformational development needs pages and pages of intricate mathematics to express. This is not the level at which any programmer, even of the next generation, would feel happy, and furthermore it is not the level at which professional mathematicians work. The success of mathematics lies in the fact that it is able to combine a rigorous formal base with the development of powerful high level concepts and methods of discovering and communicating mathematical proofs. We must do the same for transformational programming.

The concept of expressibility and intelligibility is intimately tied up with the prospects for mechanisation which we see as the ultimate pay off for program transformation. Do not be alarmed; we are not predicting the demise of the programmer or promising fully automatic programming systems; rather we are intimating that some time in the not too distant future, the power and accuracy that computers have bought to bear on productivity in other disciplines may be applied to programming itself. We exaggerate slightly. Computers, through the medium of, for example, compilers, editors, debuggers and program analysis routines, already materially assist the programming process. However the core intellectual activity of programming, the *design* of the program or algorithm, is not mechanically assisted at all. Transformation attacks exactly this central activity, and being formal and syntactically expressed is suitable for mechanisation.

Several different approaches to mechanisation are being explored. The high road consists of viewing the problem as a problem in Artificial Intelligence and attempting to construct a fully automatic system that accepts a high level specification as input and, without further user intervention, produces an efficient program. Many people, including the author, have had much fun constructing such systems and much has been learnt about the problems of search and the power of heuristics, but such systems will only become remotely practicable when solutions are found to many fundamental problems in Artificial Intelligence.

At the other end of the scale it is relatively simple to construct transformation checkers. Such systems rely totally on the user to select what transformation to apply next, but they do relieve him of many clerical burdens and ensure that the transformations are correctly applied. The problem is that for any moderate sized transformational development the number of steps needed, if all the steps are at the level of the fundamental rules of the system, becomes inordinate and difficult to comprehend.

The most promising medium term prospect lies in the development of, so called, *meta language* systems. These represent the middle way. The intelligence to guide transformational developments is still expected to come from the user but he is given structured high level ways of conveying his intentions to a system that is responsible for seeing that these are correctly carried out. The basic idea of such systems is that a separate language, the meta language, is used to describe transformations that are to be performed on programs written in the object language. Thus if the meta language is a full language, possessing function definition capability, transformations can be expressed in a structured way with the lowest level operators of the meta language corresponding to guaranteed meaning preserving operations, and the higher level, more meaningful, operations being constructed out of these.

Work at Imperial College has developed a system for transforming Hope programs that also uses Hope as the meta language. In this system the six rules of the unfold/fold systems become Hope (meta language) functions that operate on Hope (object) programs represented as Hope data structures. Out of these primitive operations more powerful transformation operators can be built using the normal function definition capability. The trick is to ensure that these defined operators inherit the correctness preserving nature of the operations on which they are based. In Hope this can be achieved using the module and typing mechanisms. The Hope data type used to represent Hope object programs, together with the basic operators, are formed into a module from which only the correctness preserving operators are exported. These operators are the only way programs can be altered. Thus the system designer or user is free to define any new operation in terms of the ones provided, secure in the knowledge that there is no way he or she can conspire to produce an incorrect program.

A range of second level operations can be identified and programmed in the meta-language, for example tactics to combine loops or convert recursion to iteration. Each such tactic is built up from the lower level tactics via the normal function definition mechanisms of Hope. On application each tactic either succeeds or fails; if it succeeds it also returns an altered program guaranteed equivalent to the original, if it fails it is an indication that the attempted transformation is inapplicable for some reason. It is important to note that there is no way an incorrect program can be produced.

Thus a transformation plan emerges as a structured Hope meta language program that is understandable, communicable and machine checkable. The Hope meta language program provides in a real sense a formal and precise notation in which to express the *design* of a program. This has important consequences not only for initial program development but also for program modification and maintenance.

If, after a program has been successfully developed, the specification from which it was derived is retained along with the meta-language program, then any subsequent modifications or enhancements can be performed on the specification. Because of the nature of specifications, this should result in fewer errors being introduced than is normally the case when complex executable code is modified. The old meta language program can then be applied to the new specification. It is to be hoped that, since the meta language program encapsulates the higher level ideas behind the design of the program, it will still be applicable to the modified specification. If it is, then no further work has to be done. If not, the worst that can happen is that the system fails to produce an acceptably efficient program from the specification. This is an indication that the modifications made are substantial enough to require a rethink of the design, and these can be expressed as modifications to the meta language program necessary to achieve a successful transformation.

SPECIFICATION TECHNIQUES

The essence of a specification is to say *what* is to be computed, not *how* it is to be computed. Specification techniques are a science in themselves, here we shall confine ourselves to a few simple illustrative examples.

In a functional language the forms that one can write are restricted to facilitate the construction of efficient interpreters. One route to languages of greater expressive power for use in specification is to remove some of these restrictions. For example, what we can write on the left hand sides of equations in Hope is severely limited. If we remove some of these restrictions we can write equations that define functions *implicitly* rather than explicitly.

For example, given that integer multiplication is defined as the Hope function `mult`, one could simply define the division function, `div`, thus

```
mult(div(n, m), m) = n
```

Such a specification can be transformed to a directly executable version using the standard manipulation rules. It is interesting to note that such specifications can also be executed, but require more sophisticated, and less efficient, interpretation regimes than are currently used for functional languages.

For any particular domain it is often possible to develop specialised specification languages often employing tabular syntaxes. One route to such languages is to regard them as syntactic extensions to an underlying functional language, and to use transformation techniques to convert them to efficiently executable programs.

OTHER LANGUAGES, OTHER TOOLS

Transformation is a general technique and has also been applied to many other styles of languages than the functional ones. Chapter six describes transformation techniques for FP (another functional language). Transformation techniques and systems based on conventional procedural languages have also been extensively studied. The fundamental nature of these languages make it difficult to establish very powerful transformation methodologies.

In contrast, transformation techniques have been very successfully applied to the other main class of declarative languages, the logic programming ones. The unfold/fold methodology can be directly translated into logic programming terms, and all the same derivations can be performed on logic programs as on functional ones. Furthermore one can use the full descriptive capability of unrestricted First Order Predicate Calculus for a specification language, and transform these specifications into efficient Horn clause logic programs.

The mathematical well foundedness of the declarative languages allows the construction of other useful tools besides transformation systems. For example, one can analyse functional and logic programs to assess their efficiency, check their consistency and one can also derive consequences from programs, for example inferring that the result of a computation can never be greater than some bound.

One possible vision for a future programming environment is that it will be founded on machine assisted transformation as the main program development activity, but supported by a collection of intelligent programming tools that offer material assistance to the programmer because they *understand* the developing program at a level much deeper than the current textual level at which most present day program support tools operate.

CONCLUSION

Transformation is a promise for the future not a present day practical reality. However, the current problems and costs associated with the development and maintenance of large scale complex software systems seems to point to the need for some radical solution that is not accessible via present day languages and methodologies.

The late 1980s promise to be fascinating years for workers in declarative languages. The coming together of parallel machines, mature declarative languages and transformation based programming environments means that all the, mutually supporting, components are in place for a searching appraisal of the ultimate practicality of this approach. Much needs to be done to turn promises into reality but the possible payoff is exciting.

6

A Functional Algebra and its Application to Program Transformation

Peter Harrison and Hessam Khoshnevisan

INTRODUCTION

One of the major benefits of any declarative language is the relative ease with which properties may be proved about programs, for example proving that two functions are equivalent. Theorems are normally expressed in terms of the results (objects) produced when functions are applied to arguments (objects) taken from some subsets of their domains. Thus, to prove that two functions are equal, it is necessary to show that their domains are the same and that when applied to any object in that domain, the results produced by each function are equal. In the functional style of FP, this type of reasoning may be greatly simplified in that the domains of objects need not be taken into account; recall that in FP (described in Chapter Three) all functions are defined in terms only of a few primitive functionals (the Program Forming Operations, PFOs) and functions. Proofs are then constructed using the rewrite rules associated with the functional algebra, i.e. from its axioms. Any consistent set of axioms is valid for defining such algebra, but the axioms of FP are chosen so that when each side of a functional identity is applied to an object, the resulting equation is known to hold at the object level. An immediate application of such a functional algebra is in transformation systems, enabling functional programs to execute rapidly, overcoming the significant obstacle to the advancement of functional languages which has been their poor run-time performance on conventional machines.

One advantage of FP definitions that are not explicitly recursive is that we can reason about the function directly, using the algebraic rules which apply to the primitives of the FP system that we are using. Also, provided that the primitives and PFOs can be implemented iteratively, the (untransformed) execution of functions defined without explicit recursion will be more efficient than that of the recursively defined counterpart.

As we have seen in chapter three, many common functions may indeed be expressed in a non-recursive form which can immediately be translated into a loop at the object level for implementation on a von Neumann computer. Furthermore, there is a large class of recursive programs which have equivalent non-recursive functional expressions. These are called 'linear' functions and often can be automatically translated into loops - the equivalent iterative form. Moreover, there are also many non-linear FP programs which can be transformed automatically into equivalent linear programs, and then compiled into iterative form.

It is the FP algebra which provides a formal basis for program transformation, and so facilitates its automation. Conventional transformation techniques prescribe algorithms for transforming functions when applied to certain arguments. The transformation strategy in FP is based upon theorems which state identities between functional expressions. A transformation is then simply an instance of the application of a theorem.

In this chapter, we use the notation defined in Chapter Three, and first illustrate the power of the algebra in some examples. We then show how non-recursive solutions for recursively defined functions can be obtained through expansion theorems and give applications of the algebraic methods in the transformation of various classes of functions into iterative form.

THE FP ALGEBRA OF PROGRAMS

If you are familiar with the concept of the field of real numbers (objects) under the composition rules of addition and multiplication (functions) which possess the properties such as associativity; then you are familiar with the well-known algebra that follows. In the same way, a set of axioms which are not self-contradictory may be defined on a set of functions under composition rules given by a set of functionals. From these axioms, it may be possible to establish, as theorems, further properties about the sets of functions and functionals, i.e. an algebra may be defined. Through the algebra, relationships between functions may be established as identities, independent of the domain of objects to which they are applied. The two sides of such an identity yield an equation at the object level for every argument to which they are each applied (possibly giving the undefined result, bottom). Thus the functional algebra provides a more general, higher level of reasoning, in which quite powerful arguments can be expressed and results deduced. Note that *any* set of axioms could be chosen provided they are consistent, but in order that the resulting algebra be useful, the axioms should not contradict known properties of conventional functional languages when applied to objects. Thus, for example, we would not choose for an axiom the statement

```
f∘[g,h]  =  [f∘g,  f∘h]
```

for all functions f,g,h, since for object x, it is not true in general that

    f:<g:x, h:x> = <f:(g:x), f:(h:x)>

(On the left hand side of the above equation f takes two arguments whereas on the right hand side f only takes one argument.) However, we can and do choose

    [g,h]∘f = [g∘f, h∘f]

Consistent axioms of the FP functional algebra have been given by John Backus, although the set has not been shown to be exhaustive. When applied to an arbitrary object, each is duly seen to yield an equality which is known to hold. As a simple example of the use of the FP algebra in formal reasoning, we first prove the equivalence between the recursive and non-recursive definitions of factorial given as follows,

    def f = eq0 → $\overline{1}$; *∘[f∘sub1, id]

    def ! = (*)∘iota   (where *:<> is defined to be 1).

We have by definition that iota = eq0 → null; ar→[iota∘sub1,id] and FP laws stating that for all functions f, g, h,

    (\f)∘ar∘[g,h] = f∘[(\f)∘g,h]

(This is easily checked from the definition of \)

and for function p,

    f∘(p → g; h) = p → f∘g; f∘h

(easily checked from the definition of →.)

Thus,(*)∘iota = eq0 → (*)∘null; (*)∘ar∘[iota∘sub1,id]

                = eq0 → $\overline{1}$; *∘[(*)∘iota∘sub1, id]

and writing ! for (*)∘iota gives ! = eq0 → $\overline{1}$; *∘[!∘sub1, id]

                                                    QED

As a second example, consider the function h which returns the length of the concatenation of two sequences. Crudely, we might define h = len∘cat where len computes the length of its sequence argument, and cat concatenates two sequences. Explicit definitions of len and cat may be found in Chapter Three. More generally, consider the definitions

    def f = p → q ; F(f)
    def g = r → s ; G(g)
    def h = f∘g

We wish to determine properties of the functionals F and G for which we can derive an optimised version of the function h. If we have (Fu)∘(Gv)=H(u∘v) for some functional H and function variables u, v, and also p∘G(g)⊃r, then by the laws of the functional algebra, we may easily prove that

$$h = r \rightarrow f{\circ}s \; ; \; Hh$$

(Note: given functions a,b then $a{\supset}b$ if and only if $a:x=T$ implies $b:x=T$ for objects x)

The composition, h, is therefore defined in simple recursive form, with no mutual recursion.

In the example of the length of the concatenation of two lists, $p=null$, $q=\bar{0}$, $Ff=+{\circ}[\bar{1}, \; f{\circ}tl]$, $r=null{\circ}1$, $s=2$, $Gg=al{\circ}[hd{\circ}1,$ $g{\circ}[tl{\circ}1, \; 2]]$. Thus,

$$
\begin{aligned}
(Ff){\circ}(Gg) &= +{\circ}[\bar{1}, \; f{\circ}tl]{\circ}al{\circ}[hd{\circ}1, \; g{\circ}[tl{\circ}1, \; 2]] \\
&= +{\circ}[\bar{1}, \; f{\circ}g{\circ}[tl{\circ}1, \; 2]]
\end{aligned}
$$

by definition of $\bar{1}$ and the identity $tl{\circ}al{\circ}[u, \; v]=v$

$$= Hh, \text{ defined by } +{\circ}[\bar{1}, \; h{\circ}[tl{\circ}1, \; 2]]$$

It is also easily checked that $p{\circ}G(g) \supset r$. This instance of the above result was first obtained as an application of the transformation methodology described in Chapter Five. The simplicity of the result, and its application to a particular example, illustrates the value of reasoning at the function level rather than having to deal with the domain of objects, using the generally applicable laws and theorems of the FP algebra. However, true though this is, it might be pointed out that a more sensible FP function to compute the length of a sequence is $f=(/+){\circ}(\alpha\bar{1})$ and to concatenate two sequences is $g=(/al){\circ}ar$. Such definitions are not only elegant, but are also easily implemented as loops at the object level directly without transformation.

EXPANSION THEOREMS AND OPTIMIZATION THROUGH TRANSFORMATION

The power of the algebra has been further developed and exploited by Backus, who introduced the *linear* class of functions. Broadly speaking, a linear function is one that generates a sequence of function calls which grows in a linear manner, and so executes in linear time with respect to the magnitude of its argument. For example, functions called tail recursive, where the recursive call is the last code to be executed, are linear, as is any function with a comb-shaped reduction graph, (see Chapter Eight for an explanation of reduction graphs), such as factorial. However, a function with a balanced tree for its reduction graph is non-linear — the Fibonacci function for example.

In the FP formalism, a linear function f has the definition

$$f = p \rightarrow q \; ; \; H(f)$$

for fixed functions p, q and *linear functional form* H defined, by the property that for all functions a, b, c,

$$H(a \rightarrow b \; ; \; c) = H_1(a) \rightarrow H(b) \; ; \; H(c)$$

for some functional H_1, called the *predicate transformer of H*. Functions for some functional H_1, called the *predicate transformer of H*. Functions defined by linear functional forms can be shown to satisfy the Linear Expansion Theorem, which may facilitate the subsequent derivation of loops at the object level. The expansion theorem asserts that given object x as argument, $f:x = (H^i q):x$ where i is an integer determined by x and the predicate transformer. (Specifically, i is the least integer such that $(H_1^i p):x = T$). Thus, for the application of f to x, f can be 'computed' iteratively in a loop on the domain of functions, starting with q in the 'accumulator' and applying H to the accumulator i times. Of course, in general, the increasing complexity of the representations of the sequence of functions q, Hq, $H^2 q$, ... renders this approach impractical, and further transformation is needed to derive an equivalent loop at the object level. The importance of expansion theorems in general is that they give non-recursive solutions to the recursion equations defining certain functions. Further use of the FP algebra may also derive non-recursive solutions as pure FP expressions from linear expansions.

It can be shown that the primitive forms of composition, condition and construction are linear, and that the linear class is closed under functional composition. The closedness property means that if a linear form is applied to a function argument which is itself the result of applying another linear form to a function variable, the resulting composite form is linear in the function variable. Thus the compiler can detect in many cases whether a defined function is linear, and if so determine its predicate transformer.

For example, any form which is built up from the PFOs composition, construction and condition, and which has only one occurrence of its function variable argument, must be linear and can be automatically transformed into loops.

To see how this works, we first identify three *simple linear forms* (SLFs) S_1, S_2, S_3 as construction, $S_1 f = [f, a]$, and compositions, $S_2 f = f \circ b$ and $S_3 f = c \circ f$ for fixed functions a,b,c. Next we define a *composite linear form* (CLF), H as the functional composition of SLFs, $H = H_1 H_2 \ldots H_n$ where each *factor* H_i is a SLF.

Now let $r_i = (H^i q):x$ where i is the least integer such that $(H_t^i p):x = T$ and let $x_i = x$, $x_{n-1} = (H_t^i):x$ n $(1 \le n \le i)$. The idea is that, if a loop implementation exists, there should be a loop invariant which contains two variables: the current value of the loop variable and an accumulator. Thus, x_n, r_n $(1 \le n \le i)$ can be computed in a loop, giving result r_i as required.

The three SLFs given above are a small subset of the full set, which also includes condition and construction of CLFs having equal predicate transformers. But they are sufficient to illustrate the transformation of the factorial function, !, defined in FP notation as

$$! = eq0 \rightarrow \bar{1};\ times \circ [! \circ sub1,\ id]$$

We may write this as

$$! = \text{eq0} \rightarrow \overline{1}; \text{ H }!$$

where $H = H_1 \ H_2 \ H_3$ and for function variables f and a,
   $H_1 f = \text{times} \circ f$ so that $H_{1t} a = a$
   $H_2 f = [f, \text{id}]$ so that $H_{2t} a = a$
   $H_3 f = f \circ \text{sub1}$ so that $H_{3t} a = a \circ \text{sub1}$

Corresponding to each SLF H_1, H_2, H_3 the associated object-expressions of variables u, v are $E_1(u, v) = \text{times} : u$, $E_2(u, v) = $ $' = \langle u, v \rangle, E_3(u, v) = u$, and so for $H = H_1 \ H_2 \ H_3$ we can show that $E_H(u, v) = \text{times} : \langle r_{n-1}, x_n \rangle$ as in the usual loop. Since the functional composition of any two linear forms is also linear, the class of CLFs which can be transformed is very rich. The technique of transforming recursive function definitions into iterative form, is called *recursion removal*, and certain types of linear functions have been proved equivalent to WHILE loops by Kieburtz and Shultz who showed that the function

   $f = p \rightarrow q; \ h \circ [i, f \circ j]$ is equivalent to

   $f' = 1 \circ w \circ [g, \text{id}]$ where

   $w = p \circ 2 \rightarrow \text{id}; \ w \circ [h' \circ [1, i \circ 2], j \circ 2]$

Here, h' is the associative dual with respect to pivot function g. For example, if h is associative, then $h'=h$ and g is its constant unit function. This result has also been derived by Backus, using the linear expansion theorem, in a somewhat weaker but more easily understood form. Clearly then, the class of linear forms is an important one, and further research, again relying on the functional algebra, has derived theorems which facilitate automatic transformation of a significant class of non-linear functions into linear form, from which an iterative implementation may follow. Before giving this result, we first explain the term *multilinear*. Informally, a multilinear form is a functional of several function variables, which is linear in each of its arguments. More precisely, it is linear in any argument when all of the others are fixed (i.e. non-variable), and moreover, the predicate transformer corresponding to each argument does not depend on any of the fixed values assigned to the others. The function f defined by

   $f = p \rightarrow q; \ Hf$

where H is a *degenerate multilinear form*, i.e. where $Hf=M(f, f, \ldots, f)$ for some multilinear form M. For example, the Fibonacci function, defined by

   $\text{fib} = 1e1 \rightarrow \text{id}; \ + \circ [\text{fib} \circ \text{sub1}, \text{fib} \circ \text{sub2}]$

is degenerate bilinear, the associated multilinear form, M, having predicate transformers M_1 and M_2 for its two arguments, given by $M_1 a = a \circ \text{sub1}$ and $M_2 a = a \circ \text{sub2}$. The function f has an expansion, by the Linear Expansion Theorem, when H is linear, for example when the predicate transformers for the function arguments of M are all equal. When Hf is not linear, we would like to find an equivalent defining equation for f in which the form M is transformed into another multilinear form M' which does have equal predicate transformers, yielding a linear definition. Here, we just give the basic result for the bilinear case as follows:-

Let $f = p \rightarrow q$; Gff where Gfg is bilinear with predicate transformers G_1 and G_2 for f and g respectively. If

(a) $G_2 = G_1^i$ for some integer $i > 1$.

(b) There exists a functional form G' with predicate transformers G_1' and G_2', such that $G(u,v) = G'(u, G_1^{i-1}v)$, for functions u,v. (This is always satisfied if G_1 has an inverse, whence $G'(u,v) = G(x, G_1^{-1}y)$).

(c) G_1 is linear with predicate transformer G_1 i.e. for all functions a,b,c,
$G_1(a \rightarrow b; c) = G_1a \rightarrow G_1b$; G_1c.

(d) $p \supset G_1^i p$ for all integers $i \geq 0$.

Then an equivalent definition for f is

$f = l \circ g$ where $g = p \rightarrow q_0$; Hg
and $G''(g) = G'(l \circ g, i \circ g)$, $q_0 = [q, G_1q, G_1^2q, \ldots, G_1^{i-1}q]$ and the functional form H is linear with predicate transformer $H_1 = G_1$, defined by

$Hg = [G''(g), G_1(l \circ g), \ldots, G_1((i-1) \circ g)]$

One prime example of this result is the transformation of the Fibonacci function given by:

$f = le1 \rightarrow \bar{1}$; $+ \circ [f \circ sub1, f \circ sub2]$

which transforms into:

$f = l \circ g$ where

$g = le1 \rightarrow [\bar{1}, \bar{1}]$; $[+, 1] \circ g \circ sub1$

By application of the linear expansion theorem for the linear form H given by $Hg = [+, 1] \circ g \circ sub1$, with $H_1a = a \circ sub1$ for function a,

$g:x = [+, 1]^i [\bar{1}, \bar{1}]:x$ for the least i s.t. $(H_1^i le1):x = T$,

i.e. s.t.x−i ≤ 1

i.e. i = x−1

Thus $g:x = [+,1]^i:<1,1> = [+,1]^{i-1}:<2,1>$
$= [+,1]^{i-2}:<3,2> = \ldots$

This reflects the usual way of implementing the Fibonacci iteration using two accumulators. (from which the logarithmic-time version can also be automatically generated).

Further optimisation is often possible for a set of mutually recursively defined functions. When combined with the linearisation techniques used in the previous example, some powerful optimisation becomes possible. Dijkstra's FUSC function satisfies the appropriate conditions and can be converted into iterative form. Denoting 'divide by two' by d, s=sub1 and p=add1, FUSC is defined by

FUSC = le1 $\rightarrow$ id; even $\rightarrow$ FUSC∘d; +∘[FUSC∘d∘p,FUSC∘d∘s]

The theorem gives FUSC = 1∘g where

$$g = \text{le1} \rightarrow [\text{id},s];$$
$$\quad \text{le2} \rightarrow (\text{even} \rightarrow [L_0g,s]; [M_0g,s]);$$
$$\quad \text{even} \rightarrow [L_0g,M_1g]; [M_0g,L_1g]$$

where L_0g = 1∘g∘d, L_1g = 2∘g∘d∘p,

M_0g = +∘g∘d∘p, M_1g = +∘g∘d

Thus the last branch of the definition for g (argument 2) becomes

$$\text{even} \rightarrow [1,+]°g°d; [+,2]°g°d°p$$

This reflects precisely the iteration of Dijkstra, and since the function is readily recognisable as linear in this form, the corresponding loop in an imperative programming language could be generated by the compiler.

CONCLUSION

This introduction to an algebra of programs or functions has tried to show some of the advantages of formal reasoning at the function-level. In contrast, the functional programming languages like Hope based upon it require that any formal reasoning be conducted in terms of mappings over the domain of objects to which the functions of interest are applied. Such domains are often of no interest in their own right, but rather tend to serve as a means to an end, perhaps even obscuring the main line of reasoning. Using the functional algebra, the reasoning 'moves up' to the function level, and properties of an auxiliary domain need not be taken into account. Thus, many properties of functions can be expressed and derived more elegantly often with greater generality. Moreover, such reasoning may be conducted in the same linguistic system as that used to write programs (viz. FP in this chapter) — of great potential to the programmer. We have seen how the power of expression and generality of the functional algebra has begun to lead to correspondingly more powerful and general transformation systems which offer a real prospect of automation. Although any conclusions are equally expressible in and applicable to the object-oriented functional languages, it is hard to see how some of the more complicated general statements could have been derived at the object level. The transformation theorems of Kieburtz, Shultis and Harrison, which are given in terms of the structures of the functionals defining the recursive functions, are examples.

7

Realistic Functional Programming

Ian Moor

REAL FUNCTIONAL PROGRAMMING

Descriptions of new programming methods have to be given with short examples. Unfortunately this means that there is still no reason for believing that functional programming is more than just an academic toy. Is it useful for anything larger than treesort? What about formatted I/O and error handling? Is it easy to debug Hope programs? This text demonstrates that functional programming can be applied to real problems and describes some of the advantages and disadvantages of writing programs in a pure functional language. Extracts from programs are included to illustrate particular points, one being that it is easier to understand such fragments in a functional language.

A functional programming environment containing all the development tools required to make program development as easy as possible has been written in Hope. Most of the ALICE operating system is written in Hope. A programming environment differs from a collection of programming tools in that it is integrated, for example a program can be entered, tested using an interpreter, inspected and changed using an editor, and then recompiled. The most widely used programming environment is probably the INTERLISP system which provides a complete LISP programming environment on several models of mainframe and large minis and is written mostly in LISP.

INTERLISP provides a LISP interpreter, compiler, prettyprinter, structure editor and several other tools to help create, maintain and document programs. A structure editor is one which understands the form of the program and provides commands that work in terms of these, such as move to next argument; a program entry system which makes sure the program is syntactically correct as you enter it is also convenient. Hope is used as a teaching and programming language, and as well as the programming environment, a number of applications programs including games, a simple database manager, and a tax advisor have been produced.

A FUNCTIONAL PROGRAMMING STYLE

Experience has shown that a distinct 'functional programming style' develops when writing functional programs. Some of this is developed naturally, other practices need to be taught or are learned slowly. Trying to imitate conventional programming style in Hope results in complex programs which are larger and more difficult to understand than programs written from scratch. The style used with Hope is also influenced by the polymorphic typing, encapsulation and pattern matching in the language (described in chapter two).

Because functional programs have no global data (except for constant functions) each part of the program, indeed each function, must be designed and written in terms of the data it consumes and produces—in a similar way to that advocated by Jackson—and can be independently tested and then composed. Pattern matching makes it easy to check that each possible case of input data has been covered: this can be done mechanically from the typing information.

A polymorphically typed language allows a programmer to build up a library of generally useful functions which can be shared among programs. More substantial programs can also be shared: the Hope compiler uses the same parser for Hope expressions and Hope types, the type of the parser is parameterized on the type of the object to be generated.

The notion of abstract data types has been adopted by the programming community as a programming tool; for example new imperative languages such as Modula-2 provide a means of separating the definition of a data type from its implementation. By defining a data type and manipulating it only through a set of interface procedures the dependence on the implementation is localized. A proper implementation of abstract data types requires a means of hiding the implementation details while permitting access to the interface functions. Hope has a module facility which provides all functions and types defined in a module except those explicitly exported and requires a module to list all the modules it wishes to use. By implementing a data type inside a module and exporting only the access functions, details of the implementation are not visible outside the module. The type set can be implemented in this way, a definition of sets is

```
module set;
pubconst nil_set,set_add,is_in ;
pubtype set;

data set(alpha) == nil_set ++
     cons_set(alpha) # set(alpha)) ;

infix is_in : 5 ;
dec set_add : alpha # set(alpha) -> set(alpha);
dec is_in : alpha # set alpha -> truval;

--- set_add(x,nil_set)
 <= cons_set(x,nil_set);

--- set_add(x,cons_set(y,s))
 <= if x is_in cons_set(y,s)
    then cons_set(x,cons_set(y,s))
    else cons_set(y,s);

--- x is_in nil_set <= false;
--- x is_in cons_set(u,v)
        <= if x = u
           then true
           else x is_in v ;
end;
```

This module implements sets as lists of the members without duplicates; other operations defined in the module such as union may depend on the absence of duplicates so it must be impossible for users of these functions to create a set with duplicates. Because the constructor cons_set is not visible outside the module, the only way a user can make an object of type set is to use the constructor nil_set or add an item using set_add which checks if an item is already in the set before adding it. Hiding cons_set makes it impossible to construct sets directly and allows the implementation to be changed, provided that all functions inside the module are changed accordingly. This module is intended to be generally useful so the type set has been made polymorphic in the type of the items in the set.

Abstract data types have proved invaluable tools when implementing the Hope programming environment: consider the symbol table which contains all the information about functions, types and modules; one might expect that changing the implementation of this might require changes throughout the system. However, the symbol table is an abstract type with a well defined set of functions for adding and retrieving information; the bodies of these functions have to be changed if the implementation is changed, but their argument and result types are fixed and documented, as are their effects. Thus the author of the parser need know only the name and type of the function which will return syntactic information about an identifier, and changing the symbol table implementation from a list to a binary tree say, requires no change on his part.

PROBLEMS AND SOLUTIONS

Input-Output

Functional languages are based on values rather than actions: a program does not *do* something, but evaluates an expression. This is in direct contrast to conventional I/O where items are read or written at some particular point in the program's execution; since there is little constraint on the order of evaluation of a functional program even on a sequential machine, an attempt to mimic conventional I/O usually goes wrong. Hope provides a couple of functions which are meant mainly for debugging:

```
pr : list char -> void;
print : alpha -> alpha ;
```

pr outputs the string without quotes and returns an empty result (of type void) while print is an identity function which outputs its argument formatted in the same way as the value of the top level expression. Print finds its use mainly for selective debugging, where it can be inserted into the program to provide some information at selected points; pr can be used for output of messages. Although it is a function, pr does not return any information, merely an empty object. Since Hope is a functional language, it is necessary to call pr as a function and handle the resulting object. Thus the following unsightly construction is often found in Hope programs:

```
--- check(x::l)  <= x::l;
--- check(nil)  <= nil
    where dummy == pr("Input is empty");
```

This may be read as—if the argument to check is not empty, return a copy of it. If the argument is an empty list, apply pr to the string, name the value *dummy*, and return the empty list. The value of an application of *check* is exactly the same as if the *where* clause were omitted from the second equation, the only difference is the state of the output device. Apart from being unclear this relies on the assumption that even though the local variable *dummy* is not used the value bound to it will be computed, which is not true in all implementations. Rather than try to mimic conventional input-output it seems better to adopt a more functional approach, based on programs which are functions, taking external data as input values and returning as its result items which are its output.

Input

Input can be supplied to a program as one of its arguments so

```
compile : list char -> list char;
```

takes the program source in text form and produces the compiled form as text. Except for simple testing nobody wants to call a program by applying it to its input in entirety, it is much simpler just to provide the file name of the input, so the conversion function

```
input : list char -> list char;
```

which converts a file or device name into its contents as a list of characters is available. The application

```
compile(input("example.hop"));
```

will compile the contents of the named file. In a call by value implementation where arguments are evaluated before applying a function this might be expected to read the whole contents of the file into memory before compiling anything. If input were being applied to a terminal, nothing would be produced until all the data had been typed in—not much use in an editor for example! To avoid these problems input is made to evaluate lazily; characters are read only when required, if the function consuming the characters requires only a line of input at a time then that is all that is read. Writing programs to return lazy lists of characters gives a set of Unix style filters which may be 'piped' together and which run as coroutines on a sequential machine and communicating processes on parallel implementations. (Laziness is described in greater detail in the appendix.)

```
compile(prettyprint(edit(input("TTY"))));
```

or

```
"TTY" input edit prettyprint compile
```

if the functions are declared as postfix operators. In Hope lazy evaluation is *forced* by the pattern matching, enough of a lazy structure must be evaluated to determine which equation applies. For example the function isnil below has to evaluate enough of the list to be able to determine which equation matches, the matching must attempt to produce the first element of the list to determine if the list is empty. In this function the pattern for the second equation has a variable as the head so the value need not be computed completely.

```
dec isnil : list alpha -> truval
--- isnil(nil) <= true;
--- isnil(x::l) <= false
```

even when applied to an infinite lazy list only the first item is computed:

```
dec thenumbers : num -> num;
--- thenumbers(n) <= lcons(n,thenumbers(n+1));

isnil(thenumbers(1));
false:truval
```

In this example if : : were used instead of lcons the Hope system would attempt to evaluate the innermost call and produce the list of all the numbers (running out of memory) before checking if it is nil.

Lazy evaluation has an overhead, typically programs which always use lazy evaluation will run at most, half the speed of the same program evaluated eagerly, assuming the eager version terminates. The overhead is caused by the need to carry an unevaluated expression about as part of the value of a lazy expression and to test for this. The function thenumbers above has to be a lazy list otherwise it would never terminate; suppose that the first two items of this list are required, the value returned is

    lcons(1,lcons(2,thenumbers(3)))

The item at the end of the list is an unevaluated expression with the value of   held in it, (in another example this might be a large structure), and the list is of a different structure at this point, which every single list operation must be prepared to handle.

Output

The tidiest approach to output is to require a program to return as a value all the text and data that is to be output. This has the advantage of removing any calls to I/O functions from the bodies of functions and making composition of programs painless. If a program returns several different items—a compiler might return a listing and code file for example, a means has to be found to indicate the destination of these. At most one of these will need to be output to the terminal, the other will be redirected to a file in some way. The simplest method of doing this is to have a Hope program return as its value a list of pairs, of which one component is the data to be output and the other indicates its destination. Hope implementations which do not support this *tagged* list can simulate it using the available output primitives, and surrounding the outermost function with a user written *shell* to do the redirection of output. Low level I/O is done in terms of *streams*, which are returned by the functions opening external files or devices. Functions are available which read a character from their argument stream and write characters or lists of strings to a stream. These functions have side effects and require care, they are normally used only to implement higher level functions such as input which are written in Hope.

Suppose that the function main returns a list of tuples in which the first component indicates to which of two files the second is to be written, then using the function prstrlst which outputs a list of strings, the output from main is split between the terminal and FILE1.DAT.

```
dec redirect : number # number #
               (number # list char) -> void;

! output a line to file s1
--- redirect(s1,s2,(1,l)::rest)
    <= let dummy == prstrlst([l,"\n"],s1) in
       redirect(s1,s2,rest);
```

```
! output a line to s2
--- redirect(s1,s2,(2,1)::rest)
      <= let dummy == prstrlst([1,"\n"],s2) in
         redirect(s1,s2,rest);

redirect(open_out_stream("FILE1.DAT"),open_out_stream
         ("TERM"),main());
```

OTHER LANGUAGE ELEMENTS

Frequently an object which appears in the pattern of an equation is also used on the righthand side of an equation, and it is tedious and perhaps inefficient to have to type it all again, particularly if it is a large pattern. To avoid doing this a variable can be associated with the object that matches the whole of the pattern as well as some of the components. If the pattern P is used in some equation, x & P allows the whole of the matching item to be referred to as x on the right of the equation. This is called a two-level pattern and is often used when writing functions which process large structures.

Similarly, a function argument or pattern component may not need to be named if it is not used in the body of function, in which case the argument can be written as an underscore, often known as a 'dont-care' which matches anything.

A REAL INTERACTIVE HOPE PROGRAM

An example of a large interactive program is the Hope version of the Edinburgh Compatible Context Editor 'ECCE' which is used as part of the programming environment for Hope. ECCE is a line based text editor, which has been transported to many different machines and operating systems: a screen based extended version has been produced at Edinburgh. ECCE was chosen as a text editor to implement in Hope because it is an extremely powerful editor and the document describing it gives a concise and full specification of the effect of each command. The Hope version is a complete re-implementation; having decided on a representation for the text buffer, implementing the commands was just a case of translating the specification for each command into Hope, an easy thing to do in a functional language. The edit buffer is implemented as a structure, containing the file name, a list of lines above the pointer (reversed), the characters to the left of the pointer (reversed), the search string (nil unless the last command was a successful search), the characters to the right of the pointer, the lines below it and the killed lines. The example below consists of the specification of the kill command, and the equations implementing it. The first equation below corresponds to the case when pointer is at the bottom, it fails if the line is empty (l<>s<>r = nil), the current line is added to the list of killed lines, and in the second equation of the first line below (b) becomes the current one. The components of the result are explained below.

```
K               Kill (line)
Effect : the whole of the current line is deleted.
Failure condition: the file pointer is at the end of the file.

! Primitive operations have type primop  !
type primop ==
        string #         ! String parameter !
        file #           ! Input file!
        list (string)    ! Terminal input !
        -> file #        ! Modified file!
           truval #      ! Success/failure !
           truval #      ! Write out file !
           list (string) #   ! Modified terminal input !
           list (string) ;   ! Output from commands !

dec kill : primop ;

--- kill(_,f & consf(name,above,l,s,r,nil,k),cmds)
  <= if (l<>s<>r) = nil
   then (f,false,false,cmds,nil)
   else (consf(name,above,nil,nil,nil,nil,(rev(l)<>(s<>r))::k),
                    true,true,cmds,nil);

--- kill(_,consf(name,above,l,s,r,b::below,k),cmds)
  <= (consf(name,above,nil,nil,b,below,(rev(l)<>(s<>r))::k),
                    true,true,cmds,nil);
```

Getting the interactive part to work proved more difficult. The editor must read and parse a line of input (the commands) and read any input requested by the command, writing any output produced by the command. Unlike batch-mode programs, the sequencing of input output in a text editor is crucial, a compiler is free to collect error messages and output them when it likes, but an editor has to reply promptly to any command. The main function of ECCE takes a lazy list of lines from the terminal and returns a lazy list of structures as output. The elements of these structures reflect the current state of the editor and correspond roughly to the variables of a procedural language. Each element of the output list consists of:

> The buffer being edited in its current state
> A list of lines to be output to the terminal
> The rest of the terminal input lines (as a lazy list).
> A boolean indicating whether the last command failed.
> A boolean used to request that the buffer be written out.

A short top-level function consumes this list, writing the output to the terminal, and the buffer to a file if requested. The main function ensures proper interleaving of input and output by causing only one item at a time to be removed from the list of input lines and producing a list of output before the next line is input. The last of the lines output when a sequence of commands has been executed is a newline followed by a >, ECCE's prompt.

The main loop of the editor, slightly simplified is

```
! If input has ended stop
--- commands(nil,TheFile) <= [(f,true,false,nil,nil)];
! An empty line on input prints the current line
```

```
! and then obeys the rest of the input commands
--- commands(nil::Lines,TheFile)
 <= lcons(printl(nil,TheFile,nil),
          commands(Lines,TheFile));
```

```
! The first line of input is non-empty - parse it

--- commands((Line1 & (_::_))::Rest,TheFile)
 <= let (action,back,ok) == parse_command(Line1)
```

```
! If the parser returns an error then complain
    in lcons((TheFile,true,nil,[('?'::Line1)<*>"\n"]),
       if not(ok)
         then   commands(lcons(back,r),f))
```

```
! Otherwise apply the command
        else
         let (File1,success,writeo,Rest1,out) ==
                do(Action,TheFile,Rest,nil) in
! And return any output
          lcons((File1,success,Rest1,
                     out<>( if not(success)
                            then ["*failed*\n"]
                            else nil)
                   <> ["\n>"]),commands(Rest1,File1));
```

The function `parse_command` parses the first of the lines of text passed to `commands` and returns a function `Action` and the rest of the input lines. If the command parsed correctly the function is applied to the file and the rest of the input. The function returns a new file and some lines of output (possibly none). If it indicates that it failed, the message '`*failed*`' is appended to the lines of output.

DEBUGGING HOPE PROGRAMS

While type checking can catch a great many potential bugs in a Hope program, there will almost always be some that slip through. Either the program will not behave as expected, or it will fail, most likely with the message `no matching equation`. It is perfectly possible to check at compile time that all cases for a function are covered by the equations, but a programmer may not intend to cover all cases. Providing an equation covering a particular case which should not arise may be difficult in cases such as the head of a nil list where there is no sensible result that can be returned. All that a programmer can do is to output an error message and stop—so why not have the implementation do it? A useful utility is a checking program (like the UNIX tool LINT for C programs) which finds parts of a program which may be wrong, such as missing cases in a function definition. Another cause of mistakes can be overlapping equations for a function, the original language proposal does not require that equations must be non-overlapping. A frequent mistake by beginners is to define a factorial by cases as

```
--- fact(n)  <= n*fact(n-1);
--- fact(0)  <= 1;
```

The language does not specify the order in which the equations are searched, in most implementations the first equation will always match and an infinite recursion results. Formal argument names are not declared in Hope, so a misspelling can turn a constructor with no arguments into a variable which matches all cases (e.g. Nil for nil in isnil above.) Opinions differ about overlapping equations: either they should be forbidden or the matching can be performed so that the least general cases are tried first (which would make the fact function above work correctly). The first solution is preferable, if less convenient, because referential transparency is preserved, the program is clearer, and pattern-matching is simpler and easier to do in parallel. The possibility of errors remaining undetected is also reduced if overlapping equations are flagged as errors. Using types with a large number of constructors (the type char for example) when no overlapping is allowed becomes rather tedious: a function on characters like is_letter will have to be defined on all 128 (or 256) characters. To avoid this a special notation for 'all cases not specified for this argument' has been proposed; this could be expanded by the implementation to a sequence of non-overlapping equations.

Debugging a program is easier when running it on an interpreter, since the program source is available for display when tracing execution. This is particularly useful for functional programs when data structures are expressed in terms of source functions. Interpreters execute programs slower than compilers, so a compiler-interpreter pair which accept the same syntax allow programs to be debugged on the interpreter and then compiled for extra speed when correct.

Because a functional program has no variables in the conventional sense, it is impossible for an incorrect program component to alter variables used by another and cause this second, correct routine to appear to be incorrect. Therefore looking at the arguments of a function returning an incorrect value or failing is all that is needed; a tracing facility will provide most of the information required to find the error in the program logic. At the very least, an implementation should provide the ability to select which function is traced, displaying the function's arguments on call and the value returned. Because functions may have many or large arguments, it is very useful to be able to select which arguments are displayed and the format of the displayed information.

THE PROGRAMMING ENVIRONMENT

A programming environment must provide at least the facilities to enter, run, modify and store permanently programs in its associated language. It can hide the underlying operating system from the language user, who can use it on different single or multi-user systems without having to know how to enter the environment. APL systems try to provide this, and the INTERLISP environment contains just about everything a LISP programmer might want or need. Some INTERLISP programmers never see the operating system, even reading their electronic mail from inside the LISP system.

WHAT THE PROGRAMMER SEES

The Hope programming environment appears to the user as a Hope interpreter with some extra built-in functions and commands. Programs can be entered merely by typing them in, and expressions are evaluated when they are entered. Two other ways of entering programs are provided, to make entering large correct programs easier. Either a *syntax-directed* entry system can be invoked, or a conventional text editor can be called with an empty buffer which is passed to the parser on exit; the parser has also been modified for interactive use to allow error correction with the minimum of effort.

SYNTAX DIRECTED ENTRY

It is always annoying when a compiler or interpreter points out something missing or not allowed; if it can detect this why can't it correct the error instead of skipping input and complaining? There are error correcting compilers which try to 'second guess' the programmer and insert missing items or ignore extra rubbish; the problem is that when they guess wrong they produce a program which does something different to the original—it is much better to prevent the programmer from making the mistake in the first place.

This is just what syntax-directed program entry systems try to do. At any place in a program, in most languages, there are only a few items which can correctly be entered at that point and the user can be presented with this choice and prevented from typing anything else. In some languages such as LISP and Micro-Prolog, which have a sparse syntax, such a system can do little except make sure that the brackets balance, but when there are more keywords and punctuation these provide guidance for the programmer. On entering this sub-system, the user is provided with a choice of Hope statements: data statement, declaration, equation etc., and can select one of these with a single keystroke. Depending on the choice of statement, the initial keyword is displayed followed by the choice at that point,—in the case of an equation, either a constant definition or function definition. Now the user must provide the name of the constant or function, which cannot be chosen from a menu since the number of choices is too big, although the identifier must have been declared and be an alphanumeric or operator symbol. Once a function name has been entered an argument list is required and so on; provided such a system runs with sufficient speed it can make program entry convenient and error free. Unfortunately it is not possible to type check a Hope expression as it is entered, so typing errors will be detected only at the end of the equation or expression.

PROGRAM CHANGES USING AN EDITOR

Editors which know at least something about the language of the file which they are editing are very useful; a 'move to matching word' where a 'word' is a language keyword or bracket is much more convenient than manually counting brackets. Being able to move and make changes in terms of the parts of the language rather than text items can reduce the number of commands (and mistakes) when editing a program.

Editors which work totally in terms of a language can have problems: consider changing the Pascal

```
WHILE  P  DO  E;
            to
REPEAT  E  UNTIL  not  P  ;
```

using such an editor. In a text editor the first step would probably be to change the **WHILE** into a **REPEAT**, but this makes the program incorrect syntactically which a fully structure-based editor would probably not allow. Conversely, if E and P are several lines each a single command to exchange two statements will perform the rest of the change much more easily on a structure editor.

The best approach is to allow both syntax-based editing and text editing in the same editor. The EMACS text editor can be customised for the syntax of a particular language by writing procedures in a version of LISP which accesses the text and can call editor primitives. These procedures can be associated with keys or edit commands; and are written to do the parsing necessary and then call the editor primitives. Such editors store the program as text and re-parse it when required, alternatively the program can be parsed and stored as the structure output by the parser, a syntax tree. Editing in terms of the program is then done by changes to the tree; in the Pascal example above the first step in the change would be to exchange the two branches of the tree representing the **WHILE..DO** statement. Other changes to the text can be made by converting the tree back to text, changing the text and reparsing the altered text.

The second approach with the program stored as a syntax tree has been adopted. As an alternative, conversion of part of the program to text can be done to allow ECCE to alter part of a program, such as a text string. The structure editor also assists in correcting errors in programs entered without the help of the syntax directed entry system, when working interactively.

When the parser detects an error, like most parsers, it tries to produce a sensible error message and reach a state where it can make sense of the rest of the program. Usually error recovery involves ignoring input up to a particular symbol—end of statement in many compilers, or assuming that a missing item has been found and carrying on from there; a careful choice of symbols to skip to or insert can mean that most of the rest of the program gets checked. In an interactive environment there is some scope for the user to make corrections when the error is found. The parser for the Hope environment was designed with this in mind. Error recovery never ignores characters, but retains them and inserts the text into a special node in the syntax tree produced for this part of the program. This node is recognised by the structure editor and by the deparser which converts trees back to text. The deparser inserts the text from the error node inside double question-marks into the output—providing an indication of where the error was detected—and the structure editor calls the text editor to handle these nodes. When the parser is being used interactively and finds an error it outputs an error message, calls the structure editor to allow corrections, and then attempts to reparse the corrected program. Type errors are handled in the same way, except that there are no nodes containing text in the trees being handled by the type checker. The dialog after a simple error appears below, with the output italicised. The editor insert and delete commands would probably be replaced by function keystrokes.

```
---  fact(succ(n))  <=  n+1)*fact(n);
%HOPE-ALICE Compiler unexpected symbol
---  fact(succ(n))  <=  n+1??)??*fact(n)  RHS
n+1??)??*fact(n)  TEXT_EDIT
n+1??)??*fact(n)  i/(/d/?/*
(n+1)*fact(n)  %reparse
---  fact(succ(n))  <=  (n+1)*fact(n)
```

where a syntax error is repaired by

> Selecting the right of the equation.
> Calling the text editor.
> Inserting a parenthesis and deleting the '?'s.
> Telling the editor to save the changes and reparse.

IMPLEMENTING THE ENVIRONMENT

Hope programs are stored not as text but as a tree-like structure which is an abstraction of the syntax, together with type information relating to the identifiers declared in the program or built-in. After type checking, the structure representing each equation has the type associated with that node; types are also represented by a structure reflecting the syntax, which is similar to, but simpler than, the expression syntax in Hope. Hope allows users to define their own operators (prefix, infix and postfix) and to extend

the syntax of the language partially by declaring distfix operators which
consist of new keywords interspersed with the operands:

```
distfix search _ for _ ;
dec search : list alpha # alpha -> truval ;
--- search nil for x  <= false ;
--- search u::v for x <= if u = x then true
                           else search v for x ;
search [1,2,3,4] for 2 ;
```

syntax information for identifiers is also stored in the symbol table, a simple
flag indicates if an identifier is an operator, but distfix operators must also
have their complete syntax stored, their declarations are converted to a form
of BNF representation which is also stored in the symbol table. The standard
syntax of the language is also represented in this way, and the distfix
representations are added to the pre-defined syntax. for example

```
syndef([term(lparen),nonterm(expression),
        star([term(comma),nonterm(expression)],
        term(rparen)])
```

represents a parenthesised list of expressions: left parenthesis, expression,
zero or more comma, plus expression and a closing parenthesis. Here lparen
represents the string '(', while expression is a function which parses an
expression, syndef, term, nonterm and star are constructors of the
syntax type. This structure representing the syntax is used by all functions
which need to know about Hope syntax down to the level of function and
infix operator application, and the parser, syntax directed entry program,
editor and the deparser all operate by *interpreting* this structure and using
the terminal symbols as input, prompts or output accordingly.

The *pipe* function composition described above provides a skeleton for the
environment, input from the terminal is lexed, parsed, type checked and
consumed by the interpreter. Each of these components may call others
depending on the input they receive, the lexical analyzer recognises commands
to load existing files or to call the text editor to return a list of lines, the
parser may call either of the editors to repair errors or the syntax-directed
entry system and the type-checker may also call for error repair. The
interpreter is the main command loop of the environment. Functions are
provided in the symbol table, some in their own modules, which give the
Hope programmer access to components of the environment and allow the
writing of *command scripts* in Hope. The meta-language transformation
system supported by the environment is controlled by exactly such programs
which describe how to convert one program into another. Because all input
to the interpreter has been type-checked first it is not possible to write such
programs without explicit type conversion functions such as parse which
converts text to an abstract type program, and evaluate which returns
the value of a program and an expression as text; the type checking
prevents mistakes here too—such as trying to execute text.

CONCLUSION

Some beginning functional programmers cannot imagine what 'real' functional programs would look like. This chapter has attempted to give an impression of large functional programs by describing large Hope programs as well as the solutions to some of the difficulties some novice functional programmers expect to meet.

Part III
Architectures

An Introduction to ALICE: a Multiprocessor Graph Reduction Machine

Martin Cripps, Tony Field and Mike Reeve

WHY BUILD A NEW COMPUTER?

It is quite possible to write compilers for declarative languages which produce code for a sequential computer and, indeed, this has been done. However, the performance which can be achieved from such compilers is often poor in comparison with conventional languages running the same problem. As mentioned in Chapter One the conventional (von Neumann) model of computation, which forms the basis for nearly all computers and programming languages in use today, is not ideally suited to expressing, or supporting, declarative programming concepts. Declarative programs implemented on these computers spend much of their time manipulating stacks, generating and invoking closures, calling functions and reclaiming unused heap storage. The von Neumann model is more ideally suited to programs which contain loops, gotos and variables and which support destructive assignment so that data and data structures can be changed by overwriting some or all of their components in-situ. In fact, it is these very features which have led to the software problem in the first place. Although some impressive performance figures have been achieved by various implementations, declarative programs will always be outpaced by equivalent imperative programs, when run on conventional machines.

In this article we shall take a look at an alternative model of computation much better suited to supporting declarative, in particular, *functional* programming languages. The most obvious difference between the architecture described here and the conventional von Neumann architecture is that the former supports declarative languages by exploiting *parallelism*. This gives us one major bonus: the potential speed of the resulting computer is no longer completely dependent upon the speed of the individual components from which they are built. If we require more computing power, we can simply use more processors i.e. we may not have to make the individual processors run faster in order to make the machine run faster, although of course we can. This applies to many parallel machines which have been proposed; the difference here is that the underlying architecture (however large or small) in no way influences the way in which it is programmed: the only difference between executing a declarative program on a machine with one processor and the same program on a machine with a thousand processors will be the execution speed obtained.

Traditionally, parallelism is achieved in two ways: either the programmer explicitly structures his program to indicate which parts may be safely run in parallel, or a specialised compiler is used which attempts to identify this parallelism automatically. Both of these techniques rely on static (i.e. compile-time) structuring or analysis of the program. ALICE, however, supports dynamic parallelism i.e. parallelism which arises through the normal execution of the program at run time.

As we might expect, we find that conventional languages run quite poorly on this new type of architecture, again because of the mismatch between language and machine.

ALICE, the Applicative Language Idealised Computing Engine was developed at Imperial College in London, U.K., to meet this need.

PARALLEL EVALUATION OF FUNCTIONAL LANGUAGES

A program written in a functional language comprises three basic components:-

1. A set of *Data Definitions*
2. A set of *Function Definitions* and
3. A *Top-level Expression* the value of which constitutes the result of (or output from) the program.

The data definition(s) describe the 'shape' of the data which will be used by the program (this is rather like defining a set of records in Pascal, say); the function definitions describe the operations which can be performed on the data; and the top-level expression simply represents what the program is to compute i.e. it initiates some computation.

To illustrate these points, and the process of program evaluation, we shall develop a simple functional program (in Hope) which will count the number of nodes on an arbitrary binary tree. This example will be referred to throughout the rest of the chapter.

Firstly, then, we must write down our data definitions—in this case there is only one definition, namely that of a binary tree:-

```
data Tree(α)  ==  Empty  ++
                  Node( Tree(α) # α # Tree(α) ) ;
```

This states that a tree is either empty or it is non-empty and contains at least one node containing an element of type α, and two further subtrees of type tree(α). Here `Empty` and `Node` are termed *constructor* functions since they only construct (i.e. bind together) data. Note that they are implicitly defined when they appear in a data statement, and that `Empty` is a nullary (zero argument) constructor—often referred to as a *data constant*.

The symbol α used in this definition is called a *type variable*. In the definition of `Tree`, we make no commitment as to the type of the objects which can be held at the nodes of the tree. We can construct trees of characters, numbers, other trees etc. using this single type definition.

Next, we must write down the definitions of the functions which constitute the program. In this example we are interested in just one function (which we shall call `Size`) which will compute the number of nodes on a given binary tree.

```
dec Size : Tree(α) -> num ;
--- Size(Empty)
        <= 0 ;
--- Size(Node(LeftTree, SomeObject, RightTree))
        <= 1 + Size(LeftTree) + Size(RightTree) ;
```

This states that `Size` takes a tree of arbitrary type and produces a number. If the tree is empty then the result is zero; otherwise its size is one plus the sum of the sizes of the left and right sub-trees. Note the program's 'declarative' reading.

We can now make the program do something by supplying an expression to be evaluated, for example given an expression representing an arbitrary tree such as:

```
Node(Node(Empty, i<2>, Empty), i<1>,
Node(Empty, i<3>, Empty))
```

we can write down a 'top-level' expression:

```
Size( Node(Node(Empty, i<2>, Empty),
i<1>, Node(Empty, i<3>,Empty)) )
```

which asks for the size of this tree to be computed. Writing this expression as a graph, we have the situation depicted in Fig. 8.1.

To start with there is only one computation site on the graph, namely the `Size` node. The computation proceeds by evaluating this node and this evaluation is determined by the definition of the `Size` function. Referring to the definition of `Size` there are two ways to proceed, depending upon what sort of tree is supplied as an argument (`Empty` or non-`Empty`). The computational model uses the two *cases*, or *equations*, which define `Size` as *rewrite rules*. Firstly, the argument of the `Size` node is *pattern matched*

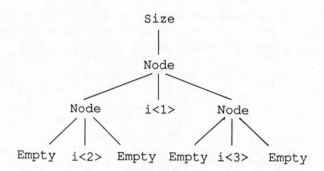

Fig. 8.1   Expression Graph for Size Example

against the left hand sides of each equation. If the given tree is `Empty` the first case will match; if it is non-`Empty` then the second case will match. Once a match has been found, a *substitution* takes place during which the part of the expression graph representing the left hand side of the matching equation is substituted by the graph representing the right hand side of the equation. In our example, the tree argument of Size will match the second equation since it is non-empty (i.e. has a `Node` constructor function at the top level) and hence the first 'rewrite' will yield:-

```
1 + Size(Node(Empty, i<2>, Empty))
  + Size(Node(Empty, i<3>, Empty))
```

i.e. as depicted in Fig. 8.2.

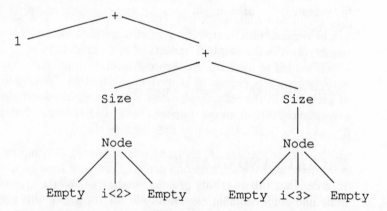

Fig. 8.2   Size Expression After First Rewrite

The term 'Expression Substitution' is often used to refer to this type of computational model, for obvious reasons.

Note that in Fig. 8.2 there are now *two* potential computational sites i.e. the two new `Size` nodes, and so the computation could proceed in parallel with separate processors operating on these two nodes concurrently. It is exactly this kind of concurrency which the ALICE machine has been designed to exploit. Observe that this concurrency has been obtained *without* assistance from the programmer: i.e. it has appeared entirely implicitly within the program. This rather curious property of functional programs has aroused the interests of computer designers as much as the languages themselves have aroused the interests of software engineers.

If we take this substitution process further we might end up with the expression graph shown in Fig. 8.3.

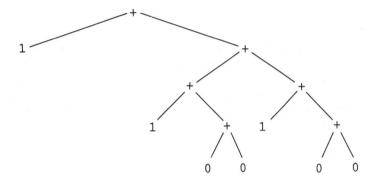

Fig. 8.3   The Size Example Fully Unfolded

The graph now contains only + operators (functions) and numbers; thus it can be *reduced* into its simplest (sometimes called 'normal') form i.e. to the number 3. It is the eventual 'reduction' of an expression to its normal form which has led to the term 'Reduction Machine' to refer to a machine based entirely upon this process of expression substitution. Observe that all we do at each step in the reduction process is to change the form of the top-level expression graph; at *no* point do we change its value or meaning.

PACKETS AND GRAPHS

In order that this rewriting process can be undertaken by a computer, we must find some suitable representation for the expression graph which is being manipulated. In the ALICE machine, each node on an expression graph is represented by a collection of data which is called a *packet*. The general packet format is shown in Fig. 8.4.

Each packet contains an *identifier* field, which distinguishes the packet from other packets in the machine; a *function* or *operator* field, which

IDENTIFIER	FUNCTION	ARGUMENT LIST (Pointers or values)	STATUS	SIGNAL SET	REFERENCE COUNT

Fig. 8.4   ALICE Packet Format

indicates which function is being represented by the packet; an arbitrary number of *argument* fields which may either be literal values or references to other packets, and a number of other fields which contain status and control information required by the machine. The number of argument fields used in the prototype machine has yet to be decided; the optimal number will be determined by analysing large functional programs. Sufficient argument fields will be available to enable most nodes to be modelled by a single packet, whilst keeping the amount of space wasted by small nodes to an acceptable limit. The identifier, function and argument fields of the packet are termed the *primary* fields; the remainder are termed *secondary* fields. It should be observed that when a packet represents part of a data structure, the function field contains a *constructor* function (for example Node or Empty) and that in all other cases it contains a *rewriteable* function i.e. one for which there exist some rewrite rules. Thus, both data structures and functions are represented uniformly using the packet scheme.

Fig. 8.5a shows the initial expression graph in the Size example represented using packets, showing only the primary fields. Fig. 8.5b shows the state of the graph after the first rewrite has been performed.

Thus, at any point in time there exist a number of packets in use in the machine, some representing data and some representing potentially rewriteable nodes on the expression graph. The amount of parallelism available is dependent upon the number of rewriteable nodes (packets) in the graph, which is potentially huge.

As a first step towards understanding the ALICE machine, we can consider the machine at an abstract level, ignoring any details of implementation. We consider ALICE as being based around an arbitrarily large collection or *pool* of processible (rewriteable) packets as shown in Fig. 8.6. Surrounding the pool are a number of processors, called *reduction agents*. These agents notionally 'dip' into the pool, extract a processible packet, rewrite the packet according to the rewrite rules of the function specified in the function field of the packet, and then return the collection of packets representing the right hand side of the rewrite rule back into the pool. Clearly, the more agents there are, the more packets we can rewrite per unit time, hence the greater the performance of the machine.

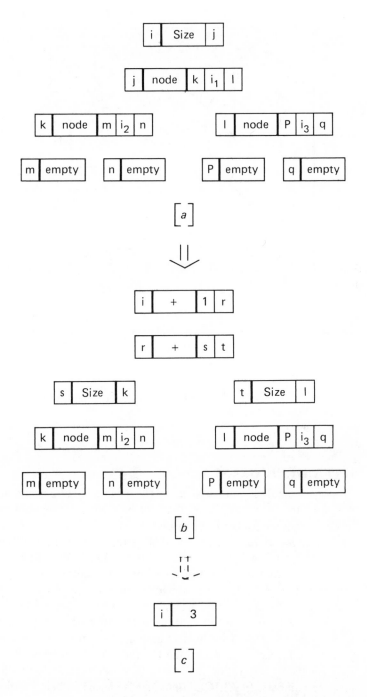

Fig. 8.5   Packet Representation of Size Example

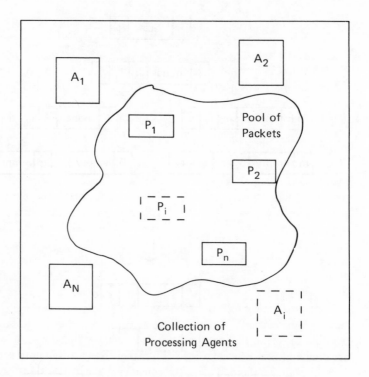

Fig. 8.6   ALICE Abstract Architecture

DATA DEPENDANCY

Ideally, we should like *every* packet in the machine to be executable. However, it is often the case that a packet cannot be rewritten because it requires the result of another packet to be available before its own rewrite can proceed. This is called *data dependency*. This effect occurs in our Size example whenever a '+' packet is generated, as in Figure 5b. Clearly, '+' cannot proceed until its two arguments have been reduced to data—in this case, to numbers. Therefore, we must provide some mechanisms for postponing the evaluation of '+' until these arguments have been reduced to number form. This is achieved in ALICE by means of a *Suspend/Signal* mechanism: when a '+' packet is picked up by a reduction agent the argument fields of the packet are inspected to determine whether the arguments are in the right form for the '+' operation to proceed. The rule here is that both arguments must be numbers. In ALICE, a number is viewed as being a special case of a constructor function, so that there are effectively as many number constructors as there are numbers. So, the test to determine if an argument is a number simply involves asking: 'is the function field of the argument a constructor function?'. If so, then the function field denotes the number.

Let us assume that when this test is performed *neither* argument is in the correct form, as is the case with the 'r' packet in Fig. 8.5b. In this example a *signal request* is left in part of the status field of both argument packets, namely 's' and 't'. This request is simply a backward pointer to the packet which requires the value of 's' and 't' i.e., it is simply the identifier, 'r'. There may be several entries within a packet, i.e. the result produced by the packet may be required by several other packets. The set of all signal requests within a packet, P, are collectively referred to as the *signal set* of P, i.e. the set of packets requiring that value of P when it is eventually produced. When a rewrite causes the function field of a packet to be overwritten with a constructor function (a '+ 1 1' packet being overwritten by the number '2', for example), a *signal* is sent to each packet listed in the signal set of that packet. To complement this, in our example, when the signal requests are left in 's' and 't' a *pending signal* count of 2 is left in part of the status field of 'r' and the 'r' packet is temporarily *suspended*. Each signal subsequently transmitted to 'r' will cause the pending signal count of 'r' to be decremented by 1. When this count reaches zero, 'r' can be reactivated and evaluated since we now know that its arguments are both numbers. Note that it is possible to set up these signal sets and pending signal counts when packets are created (as a result of a rewrite), rather than waiting until some processor tries to evaluate them. This saves considerable extra work at run time. Note also that when the result is a simple literal, as in the 's' packet in the Size example, the literal value can be copied directly into the argument field of the packet, or packets, awaiting its result. Thus in the example, the argument field referencing 's' in packet 'r' could be overwritten with the actual value of 's' (which will be 1) rather than just sending a signal to 'r'. This latter optimisation is termed *data flow* signalling, since it implies a 'flow' of data from the arguments to the operators. The signalling mechanism described earlier is termed *control flow* signalling, since there is an implied flow of control information between argument and operator. For experimental purposes, the ALICE prototype supports both types of signalling mechanism, and allows suspend and signal information to be either preset within a collection of packets when they are created, or generated *on the fly* when the evaluation of the packets is attempted.

Fig. 8.7 shows the state of the packet graph in the Size example just after the signal sets have been set up in 's' and 't'.

RESTRICTING EVALUATION

Thus far, we have placed no restriction on the rate at which packets are produced. The only evaluation restrictions which have been imposed are those which are necessary because of data dependency. Whilst this maximises the amount of parallelism being exploited by the machine, there is nothing to

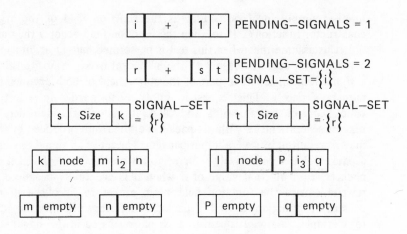

Fig. 8.7   ALICE Signalling

stop the machine from saturating its memory resources by producing more packets than there is space to hold them. The evaluation strategy is thus said to be eager i.e. 'if it can be done, then do it!'. To allow for greater flexibility in control, ALICE incorporates some extensions to the computational model by allowing for what is termed lazy evaluation. (See Appendix for more detailed description of lazy evaluation.) Unlike the eager evaluation strategy, in which packets are rewritten without regard as to whether, or when, they will be required, lazy evaluation delays the evaluation of a packet *until* its value is requested by some other packet. Thus if our Size example is evaluated lazily instead of eagerly, the 's' and 't' packets will not be evaluated until their values have been 'demanded' by the 'r' packet. Using eager evaluation, 's' and 't' can be evaluated without having to wait for these demands to be issued. In fact, lazy and eager evaluation are the two extremes of a more general evaluation strategy termed *anticipatory* evaluation. ALICE implements eager and lazy evaluation indirectly by supporting anticipatory evaluation.

GARBAGE COLLECTION

Let us now go back to the Size example and consider what happens when the first rewrite occurs. An examination of Figs. 8.5a and 8.5b will reveal that the rewriting of the original Size packet (packet i) introduced a number of additional packets (packets r, s and t) into the graph. Furthermore, packet j in Fig. 8.5a was removed ('consumed') during the rewrite so does not appear in Fig. 8.5b. So, where did packets r,s and t come from and where did packet j go to? The answer lies in the *garbage collector*. The garbage collector is that part of the machine responsible for gathering unused packets. Initially, all the packets in the machine (except for those which hold the rewrite rules and top-level expression) will be unused or *free*. As the evaluation proceeds, new packets will be required and existing packets will be released reflecting the change in structure of the expression graph being built up. Each packet contains an additional field within its control and status fields which is referred to as a *reference count* field. This contains a count of the number of packets which have an occurrence of that packet within their argument fields. Since one packet can be shared arbitrarily by many other packets, this counter can assume any value. In the Size example, the situation is rather simple: each packet has a reference count of one! This is because none of the packets are shared.

The garbage collector maintains the reference count fields of all the packets. Every time a new reference is made to some packet, P, the reference count of P is incremented. Every time a reference to P is destroyed (for example when P's value has been consumed by some other packet), the reference count of P is decremented. When the reference count of P reaches zero, no packet refers to P and so P can be *garbaged*. A complete set of free packet identifiers is maintained at all times; thus when a new packet is required, an entry is removed from this set, and when a used packet becomes garbaged, an entry is added to the set. In the ALICE machine, garbage collection takes place concurrently with the rewriting activities of the agents.

THE ALICE PROTOTYPE

The abstract computational model described above was implemented in prototype form at Imperial College using INMOS Transputers as building block processors. The Transputer is a single-chip microcomputer comprising, at present, a high-performance processor, 2Kbyte of 50ns static RAM and four 10Mbit/sec serial communication links. The Transputer is programmed using a high-level language called **occam**. The prototype machine has been designed to enable detailed instrumentation to be performed, and makes full use of the flexibility of **occam** and the INMOS Transputer to achieve this. The fact that the *microcode* of the machine is written in **occam** enables any desirable or experimental changes to be made to the microcode both rapidly and reliably. The first commercially available ALICE machines will be implemented using custom VLSI technology.

The architecture of the prototype ALICE computer is shown in Fig. 8.8. The machine consists of an arbitrary number of reduction agents ($A_1 .. A_n$), and packet pool segments ($PPS_1 .. PPS_m$) which can communicate with one another through a high-bandwidth interconnection network. A low-bandwidth distribution network also links the agents and pool segments and is used for load sharing and for maintaining the free packet identifier set described above. Also present, but not shown on the diagram, is an ETHERNET

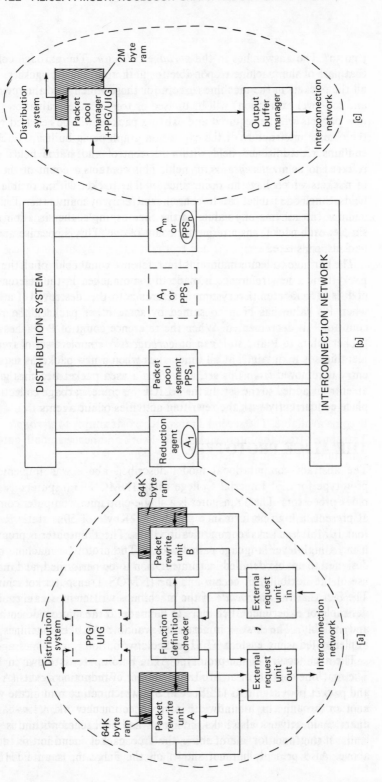

Fig. 8.8   The ALICE Prototype

controller, also attached to the networks which links to an ICL-2900 host computer which performs I/O, file handling and statistics-gathering. Each box in Figs. 8.8a and 8.8c represents one Transputer in the prototype machine.

THE PACKET POOL

In Fig. 8.8b, the packet pool is shown distributed over a number of 'intelligent' packet pool segments. This is to enable many reduction agents to have access to the packet pool at the same time, which would not be possible if there were a single shared packet store. Each pool segment contains two Transputers and two megabytes of random-access memory as shown in Fig. 8.8c. The main 'workhorse' Transputer performs two roles: firstly, it receives, processes, and responds to, messages issued by the reduction agents (a typical message might be the one quoted above: 'please tell me whether the function field of packet P is a constructor'), and secondly, it manages part of the distribution system. The distribution system circulates both the *identifiers* of all packets known to be *candidates* for processing *and* the identifiers of all free packets, throughout each device in the machine. The distribution system is in the shape of a ring and is implemented using two Transputer links and some RAM from each device. The total number of words of RAM used by the ring must be at least as large as the total number of packets in the system. Garbage collection can be performed by the packet pool segments and the garbaged packet identifiers circulated on the distribution ring as soon as they become available. The second Transputer exists simply to *decouple* the main Transputer from the interconnection network and hence smooth out external communications via the network to other devices.

THE REDUCTION AGENTS

Each reduction agent consists of two rewrite units which share a rewrite rule lookup table and links to the distribution system and interconnection network. The reduction agent layout is shown in Fig. 8.8a.

In order to maximise the utilisation of the rewrite units and to overcome any delays incurred in accessing the packet store, each packet rewrite unit supports eight *virtual* rewrite units. These are implemented as eight identical **occam** processes which are run on the same Transputer. When a virtual rewrite unit requires work it requests a processible packet identifier from the (shared) Transputer which manages the distribution ring. A message is then sent to the store segment containing the packet requesting a copy of the packet to be sent to the virtual rewrite unit. When the packet is returned, the packet is written to a local cache, and the function field of the packet is sent to the function definition checker. The checker maintains a table of function identifiers whose definitions have been cached within the rewrite units. If the function field of the incoming packet is found in this table, then a message is sent to the rewrite unit indicating that the rewrite can proceed.

If the function identifier is not in the table then a copy of the definition is requested from the packet store via the network. The packet pool contains one 'master' copy of each function definition in the program. The identifier of that function is simply the address, in the pool, of the master copy. When the definition is received, it is placed in part of the 64Kbyte cache associated with each rewrite unit, and the address at which it is loaded is added to the lookup table within the function definition checker together with the associated function identifier. Entries are thus continually added to and removed from the checker table and cache in much the same way that entries are added to and removed from conventional page tables. The entire lookup table is stored in the on-chip RAM associated with the checker Transputer.

Whilst one virtual agent is waiting for I/O to complete through the network, another virtual agent can be switched in and allocated the CPU. The objective is to overlap processing and I/O such that the CPU is fully utilised. All communication through the network is controlled by external request units which contain a small amount of discrete logic to control the addressing of the network.

THE INTERCONNECTION NETWORK

The configuration of the ALICE interconnection network is shown in Fig. 8.9.

This type of network is called a *multistage* interconnection network since it consists of a number of smaller switches arranged in layers or stages. Each of the smaller switches shown is a 4x4 crossbar switch, which is capable of coupling any of its four inputs to any of its four outputs. By appropriately selecting the individual switches of the network, it is possible to establish a communication path between any network input link and any network output link.

It will be seen that the set of paths connecting any one input link to all the output links forms a complete 4-ary tree. Thus, if there are n stages in the network, then we can construct a network of this type with 4n inputs and outputs. The ALICE prototype uses a network with three stages i.e. with 64 inputs and outputs.

Each component 4x4 switch is a custom-designed ECL device named the XS1. In order to reduce the engineering cost and complexity of the network, the data paths through the network, and hence the XS1, are high-bandwidth bit-serial lines. These lines are used both to set up a path through the network and to transmit data across the network. Furthermore, the network is asynchronous. This means that no global synchronisation clock need be distributed to the switches, and also that communication paths can be set up at any time and held for any time. Each XS1 is capable of switching in 85ns and can pass data (and a data synchronisation clock at the same time), through itself at rates of up to 150 Mbits/sec. Although the XS1s are greatly under-utilised by the Transputer links, which clock at a maximum of

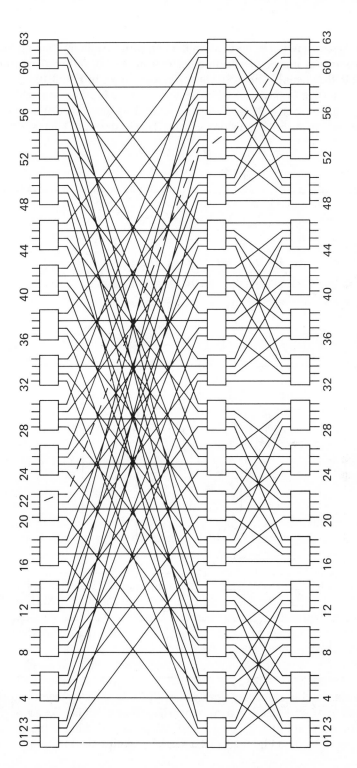

Note: Connection between input 22 and output 60 shown dotted.

Fig. 8.9   The ALICE Interconnection Network

10Mbits/sec, they can be used in conjunction with custom interfacing devices, and operated at higher speeds, in other machines or in future generations of the ALICE machine. The XS1 chip circuit is shown in Fig. 8.10.

Each agent (five Transputers with the two 64K byte blocks of store) is housed on a double eurocard PCB. Communication between onboard Transputers is achieved by direct connection of the Transputer serial links. Offboard

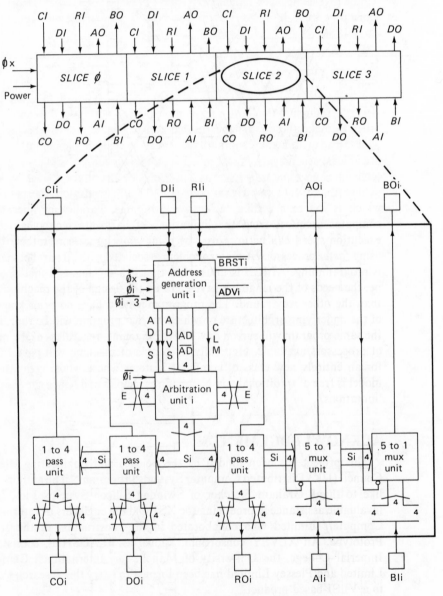

Fig. 8.10   XS1 CHIP (circuit details)

communication is handled via the network which occupies six PCBs. Each packet pool segment (two Transputers plus two megabytes of RAM) is also housed on a double eurocard PCB.

The VLSI version of the machine (which is now being developed) is expected to provide at least two orders of magnitude increase in speed over conventional computers running the same program. Because this machine will be extensible, even higher performance can be achieved by incorporating more processors into the system. The prototype machine was completed in early 1986.

CONCLUSION

We believe that declarative programming offers the most promising route towards reducing the cost and complexity of software development. In order to make these languages usable and to enable them to become more widespread within the community we must provide implementations which are at least as efficient as those of conventional languages. Clever compilation techniques go some way towards achieving the necessary efficiency, but we believe that future implementations should aim to exploit the parallelism which is inherent within declarative programs. Parallelism liberates the computer architect from the limitations of hardware technology so that execution speed can be improved by using *more* processors rather than by using *faster* processors. A major problem associated with all parallel machines is programming. ALICE is unusual in that it is a 'language first' machine, i.e. the needs of the language have dictated the design of the machine rather than the other way round. The programmer need have no prior knowledge of the underlying architecture on which his/her program will be run. Indeed, the same program will run on any ALICE machine, regardless of the number of processors available. Hopefully, this style of machine will pave the way for an entirely new class of computer systems whose whole computational model is free of traditional von Neumann principles and hence the associated limitations.

ACKNOWLEDGEMENTS

This project has been funded by the Science and Engineering Research Council (UK) Distributed Computer Systems Programme. The authors would like to thank Graham Fletcher of Swindon Silicon Systems Ltd., for his invaluable assistance in producing the XS1 and the engineers at International Computers Limited who collaborated in the construction of the ALICE Prototype. An ALVEY consortium, known as FLAGSHIP, consisting of Imperial College, the University of Manchester, International Computers Limited and Plessey Limited has been formed to carry this research through to a VLSI-based product.

9

Applicative Languages and Data Flow

Chris Hankin, David Till and Hugh Glaser

INTRODUCTION

For many years computer scientists have been concerned with the issues related to making a number of processors cooperate on a single task. Some of the most difficult problems are connected with the control of access to global resources and the lack of referential transparency in imperative languages. In recent years language designers have turned to functional languages (described in Part I) as a way of avoiding these problems. In the field of computer architecture data flow has emerged as a paradigm for closely-coupled multi-processor machines (chapter eight describes an alternative model called graph reduction); thus it is natural to consider the link between functional languages and data flow and we shall investigate this link.

The salient feature of data flow is that instead of a centralized control unit and a program counter, operations are selected for execution when their operands have been computed. Thus the flow of data between operations provides the sequencing control which would normally be provided by the program counter in a conventional 'control flow' machine. When several operators have all their operands ready, any or all of them can be performed in sequence or simultaneously, and this is what gives rise to parallelism within data flow systems. Operators can have no 'side effects': they receive a number of inputs and produce a number of outputs. There are no concepts of instruction sequencing or global memory.

Two different data flow models, pipeline data flow and token data flow, will be examined; in both models data flow programs are represented by directed graphs. The nodes of a pipeline data flow graph are used to represent processes and the arcs represent channels between processes. In this model the arcs carry streams of data between processes. There has been a substantial amount of work done on the formalization of pipeline data flow and it has formed the semantic basis for some of the work on multiprogramming using functional languages. All of the current data flow architectures, however, are based on token data flow. In this model the nodes are used to represent more primitive operations and the arcs are the channels that carry the operands and hence represent the data dependencies between operators. Approaches to token data flow differ in the rules that are used in the construction of programs. In this chapter we restrict our attention to acyclic graphs, partly because this makes the treatment more straightforward but also because we feel that this approach is more appropriate for the implementation of functional languages.

We can see some of the benefits of using data flow in the implementation of functional languages by considering a simple example:

```
dec sum_square : num # num -> num;
--- sum_square(a, b) <= a * a + b * b;
```

While this program does not specify any control information, it is clear that the plus operator requires the results of the two multiplications and that these can be evaluated independently. This information becomes explicit if we redefine the function in a formalism that highlights the data dependencies between operators. This is precisely what the data flow notation does. There are a number of research projects which are directed towards the construction of data flow computers. With few exceptions the link between data flow and functional languages has not played a major role in these projects. This is evidenced by the fact that none of the architectures have provided efficient support for higher-order functions.

In the next section we describe a data flow notation that may be used for the translation of functional programs. We then go on to describe two algorithms for the execution of data flow programs. Both of these mechanisms support the full range of facilities that are found in functional languages.

A DATA FLOW NOTATION

The notation we shall use consists of a set of five basic operator types, a function application operator and a notation for function definition. Inputs and Outputs to and from a graph are shown as arcs that are connected to the graph at one end only. The basic operators are shown in Fig. 9.1.

All data dependencies are explicitly shown in the graph, so that if two operators use the same value, they must both have an input arc that emanates from the same place. There is an explicit duplicate node that may be used to provide the appropriate number of copies of a value. The value generator is the operator used to insert literal values onto the graph at run-time; literal values include the integers, booleans and other primitive types as well as function names (see below). The switch and merge operators are used to

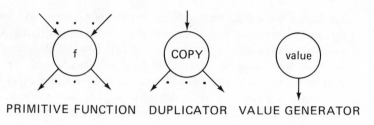

PRIMITIVE FUNCTION   DUPLICATOR   VALUE GENERATOR

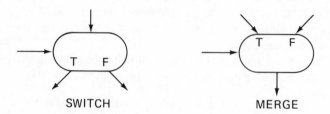

SWITCH   MERGE

Fig. 9.1 Basic Data Flow Operations

construct conditional computations. For example, the graph for the defining
expression of the Hope function:

```
dec f : num -> num;
--- f(a)  <= if P then A else B;
```

(where P, A and B are arbitrary expressions referring only to a), might
appear as shown in Fig. 9.2.

At run-time the switch uses its control input, which is a boolean, to select
one of its output arcs to receive the input value. Similarly, the merge uses
its control input to select a value from one of its input arcs. If the expressions
of the conditional had used other values from the environment, for example
if there were other parameters to the function, then the graph would require
multiple switches and merges all taking their control input from the P graph.

A graph may be defined as a function by enclosing it in a *box* (see for
example Fig. 9.5). The arcs entering the box represent the parameters of the
function and the arcs emanating from the box represent the results of the
function. The name of the function is written in the bottom left hand corner
of the box. An application of a user-defined function is represented by an
explicit apply node as indicated in Fig. 9.3.

Recursive function definitions are represented by boxed graphs containing
self-referential apply nodes. Assuming that we have a definition for factorial,
Fig. 9.4 is an example of a typical use of the apply node.

When a function has more than one parameter, the situation is slightly
more complex because the apply node only has one parameter input. The
graph of the product function:

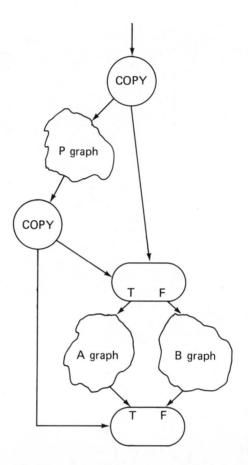

Fig. 9.2 A Conditional Data Flow Graph

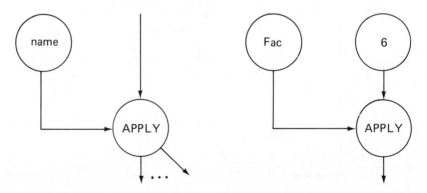

Fig. 9.3 The Apply Operator   Fig. 9.4 The Application of Fac

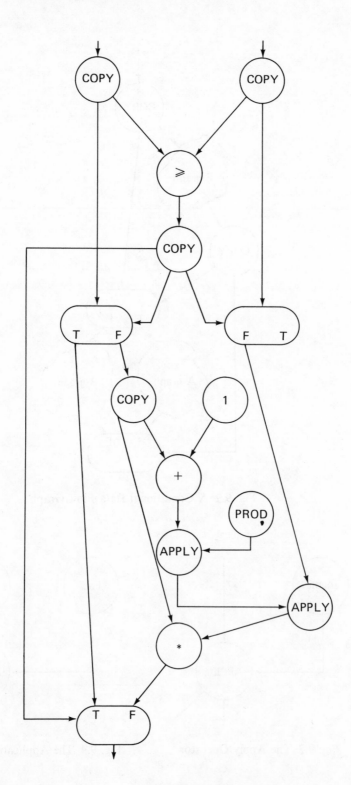

Fig. 9.5 The Data Flow Graph for the Product Function

```
dec prod : num # num -> num;
--- prod(a, b) <= if a >= b
                  then a
                  else a * prod(a + 1, b);
```

is shown in Fig. 9.5.

(Note: the T output from the right hand switch is omitted because the value of b is not required when the condition is satisfied.) Any application of prod will require the two apply nodes of Fig. 9.6.

Two questions arise:

(1) What value is produced by the first apply node?
(2) Which function name is supplied to the second apply node?

Both questions can be answered by a more careful consideration of function names. In this notation, a function name is not just an identifier but also contains information about the number of parameters required by the function and the values of any parameters that have been *fixed*. Thus the first apply node in the diagram produces a new name which has the same identifier as prod but has the additional information that the first parameter has been fixed at 2. We shall use the term *closure* to refer to such a function name that contains fixed parameters. The answer to the second question is that we connect the output of the first apply node to the name input of the second.

When the name input of an apply node carries a function that only requires

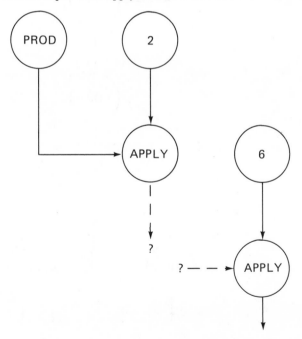

Fig. 9.6 An Application of the Product Function

one further input, the node is conceptually replaced by a copy of the function. This copy is executed using the parameter from the replaced node and the values that have been fixed by preceding apply nodes. This process corresponds to the notion of curried function application from the lambda-calculus and is much more powerful than the example suggests. For example, the name produced from an apply node need not be passed directly to the next apply but may be copied or transformed in some way first. The name produced by the first apply in the example corresponds to a single parameter function that produces the product of all values between 2 and the parameter value. We show an example of such use in Fig. 9.7.

Thus the data flow graph of the example provides a more general solution to the problem than the Hope function. However, we can produce an equivalent Hope program using lambda expressions:

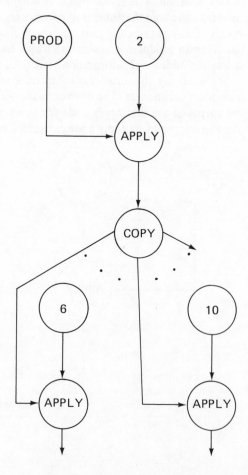

Fig. 9.7 Curried Application

```
dec prod : num -> num -> num;
--- prod(a) <= lambda b => if a >= b
                           then a
                           else a * prod(a + 1, b);
```

As a final remark on this data flow notation we note that the apply node does allow multiple outputs. This allows us to translate Hope functions that produce tuples of outputs. In this case, any *internal* apply node that produces a name will have a single output and the final apply node will have the same number of outputs as there are elements in the tuple.

DATA FLOW EVALUATION MECHANISMS

There are two approaches to the evaluation of data flow programs. One is the classical data-driven approach, which is a call-by-value mechanism in which arguments are evaluated before they are passed to a function. The other is the demand-driven approach which provides lazy evaluation. For our purposes the important aspects of lazy evaluation are that arguments are not evaluated until they are required, and if required are evaluated only once. (See the Appendix for a more detailed description of lazy evaluation.) We describe each mechanism at an abstract level within the context of the data flow notation that we have presented.

First, we define a data-driven mechanism, representing data flow instructions as follows:

A data flow instruction consists of

IDEN:	an identifier
TYPE:	a type which is one of the basic operators or apply
INPR:	an input record which has a field for each input
OUTL:	an output list which is a list of instruction identifier/input field name pairs

Each value produced from the execution of an instruction must be directed to a particular input arc of some other instruction. Therefore we need a way of uniquely identifying instructions and a way of distinguishing between input arcs. We have used a record with named fields to represent the set of input arcs and each instruction has a unique identifier. Destinations for each of the results of an instruction are specified in the output list which contains one instruction/input field pair for each output arc. The type of the instruction identifies which operation is to be performed, which in the case of value generators and primitive functions must include information about which specific instance of the class is required. An example of a data flow program in this notation is shown overleaf.

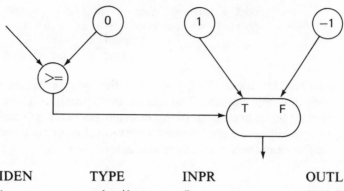

IDEN	TYPE	INPR	OUTL
1	value/0	()	(2.right)
2	>=	(left,right)	(5.control)
3	value/1	()	(5.true)
4	value/-1	()	(5.false)
5	merge	(control,true,false)	(*)

Fig. 9.8 A Simple Data Flow Graph

This is a program that returns the sign of its input, which arrives in the 'left' input field of instruction 2. As we noted earlier, outputs emanate from a particular instruction but are not directed towards any instruction. This is represented in the code by an asterisk in the output list of an instruction.

The major cycle of the execution mechanism is shown below. There may be several different instances of this cycle active at any one time and each operates asynchronously with the others:

```
FOR any instruction DO
      IF the instruction has all of its required inputs
      THEN execute the instruction
      ENDF
ENDD
```

Now we consider what is meant by 'the instruction has all of its required inputs'. This will vary according to the type of the instruction under considera-tion, and can be represented by the following expression:

```
   the type is value
OR the type is one of primitive, copy, switch, apply
   AND all fields in the input record contain values
OR the type is merge
   AND the control input field and the appropriate other
           input field contain values
```

We see that a value operation always has its required inputs, and all other operations require a complete set of inputs except for merge which requires only its control input and the selected input.

The most complex part of the cycle is to 'execute the instruction', and this may be represented as follows:

```
CASE type of instruction OF
    primitive : perform the operation using the inputs;
                FOR each instruction in the output list DO
                    put the appropriate result in the specified
                    input field
                    ENDD,
    copy : FOR each instruction in the output list DO
           put the value from the input record into the
           specified input field
           ENDD,
    value :     put the value into the specified input field;
    switch : IF the control input is TRUE
             THEN place the other input value in the
                  specified input field of the first instruction
                  in the output list
             ELSE place the other input value in the
                  specified input field of the second instruction
                  in the output list
             ENDF,
    merge : IF the control input is TRUE
            THEN place the second (true) input value in the
                 input field specified in the output list
            ELSE place the third (false) input value in the
                 input field specified in the output list
            ENDF,
    apply : IF the first input is a single parameter function
            THEN generate a copy of the function;
                 place the second input value in the input record
                 of the first instruction in the function
            ELSE IF the first input is a closure which requires
                 a single parameter
                 THEN generate a copy of the function;
                 pass the second input and the closure values to
                 the input records of the appropriate instructions;
                 ELSE generate a new closure with the second input
                      value
                 ENDF
            ENDF
ENDC;
delete the instruction;
```

With the exception of apply, the execution mechanism is straightforward. In the case of apply it is necessary to distinguish between an application that is providing the last parameter to a function or closure, in which case a copy of the function is generated ready for execution, and the other cases where a new closure is produced. The new copy of a function has to be 'knitted into' the program by setting up the input records of initial instructions with

parameter values and ensuring that the function output instructions send
their results to the correct destinations. This mechanism to 'generate a copy
of the function' is shown below:

```
create a new copy of each instruction in the function, assigning
      unique identifiers and changing the output lists accordingly;
FOR each output instruction in the function DO
      set the output list to the appropriate values from the
            output list of the apply operator
ENDD;
```

Since the program is acyclic and instructions are thus executed only once,
each instruction is deleted after it has been executed.

As an example of this process we show how the sign program would be
executed when the input is 5. Each snapshot in the trace results from
executing all possible instructions:

	IDEN	TYPE	INPR	OUTL
Step 1:	1	value/0	()	(2.right)
	2	>=	(left:5,right)	(5.control)
	3	value/1	()	(5.true)
	4	value/−1	()	(5.false)
	5	merge	(control,true,false)	(*)
Step 2:	2	>=	(left:5,right:0)	(5.control)
	5	merge	(control,true:1,false:−1)	(*)
Step 3:	5	merge	(control:TRUE,true:1,false:−1)	(*)
Step 4:	1 (The result to be output)			

In demand-driven systems the computation is controlled by a combination of
the presence of operands and a request for the result of an operation.
Effectively, a structure is imposed on the program which carries requests in
the reverse direction to the flow data. The requirement is reflected in an
extended definition of a data flow instruction:
A data flow instruction consists of

IDEN: an identifier
TYPE: a type which is one of the basic operators or apply
SOUL: a source list which is a list of instruction identifiers
INPR: an input record which has a field for each input
OUTL: an output list which is a list of instruction identifier/input
         field name pairs

The representation of the program is therefore slightly more complicated, the sign program being specified as follows

IDEN	TYPE	SOUL	INPR	OUTL
1	value/0	()	()	(2.right)
2	>=	(?,1)	(left,right)	(5.control)
3	value/1	()	()	(5.true)
4	value/-1	()	()	(5.false)
5	merge	(2,3,4)	(control,true,false)	(*)

The main execution cycle is also more complicated. Only instructions whose results have been requested are executed and then only if the required operands have been computed, otherwise the request is propagated. The mechanism is defined below:

```
FOR any instruction whose output has been requested DO
    IF the instruction has all of its required inputs
    THEN execute the instruction
    ELSE CASE type of instruction OF
            primitive,copy,switch :
                    send the request to all instructions in
                    the source list,
            merge :  IF control input is present
                    THEN IF control value is true
                            THEN send the request to the second
                                instruction in the source list
                            ELSE send the request to the third
                                instruction in the source list
                            ENDF
                    ELSE send request to first instruction
                            in source list
                    ENDF,
            apply : send the request to the first instruction in
                    the source list

        ENDC
    ENDF
ENDD
```

Only the inputs that are needed by merge are requested. The control input is requested first and then either the true input or the false input is requested, depending on the control value. The specifications for 'the instruction has all of its required inputs' and 'execute the instruction' are the same as the data-driven version except for the apply operator. The apply operator requires only its left input, the function or closure name, and is executed in the following way:

```
apply : IF the first input is a single parameter function
     THEN generate a new copy of the function
     ELSE IF the first input is a closure which requires
             a single parameter
          THEN generate a new copy of the function
          ELSE generate a new closure remembering the identifier
               of the second instruction in the source list
          ENDF
     ENDF
```

In this mechanism, a closure consists of the function name and a list of instruction identifiers that are the sources of its parameters. The parameters may thus be requested, if required, when the function is evaluated. We define 'generate a new copy of the function' as follows:

```
create a new copy of each instruction in the function, assigning
     unique identifiers and changing the source and output
     lists accordingly;
FOR each input instruction in the function DO
     set up the source list
ENDD;
FOR EACH output instruction in the function DO
     set the output list to the appropriate values from the
          output list of the apply operator;
     request the output if required
ENDD
```

This mechanism provides lazy evaluation (assuming a lazy constructor for lists) because values are computed only when they are required and once a value has been computed it will be available to any later requests. (This is because copy sends its result to all instructions in its output list, even if they have not all requested the value).

CONCLUSION

Finally, it is important to comment on the relationship between the wider objectives of data flow research and functional languages. Few of the data flow projects that are at an advanced stage were begun with functional languages in mind. The primary intention is to exploit the data flow mechanism in order to gain execution speed either for conventional or data flow languages. Thus we find that the model here described, designed to bear a close relationship with functional languages, is different from many of the other notations used; in particular a number of data flow machines do not support higher order functions in a natural way.

The traditional data flow mechanism is beginning to bear fruit in the field of high speed computation, and it is clear that the model we have described has excellent potential for the implementation of functional languages. It remains to be seen whether functional languages and data flow will form a useful partnership.

Combinators as Machine Code for Implementing Functional Languages

Brian Boutel

EXECUTING FUNCTIONAL PROGRAMS

Functional languages are a very attractive way of writing programs, but if they are to be of any use there must also be a way of executing programs written in these languages which is reasonably efficient and does not lose the advantages gained from using a functional style.

The ALICE computer, described in chapter eight, is intended to execute programs written in functional languages, exploiting the opportunities for parallelism which arise from the absence of assignment statements in languages which are based on expressions rather than imperative commands. ALICE is a graph reduction computer, which means that the program being executed is also a data structure being modified (reduced) until it becomes the desired result. This data structure has the form of a graph, that is, it consists of a number of nodes, each of which can contain a number of pointers to other nodes as well as values. Each node may have several other nodes pointing to it, and, in some graph reduction schemes, although not in ALICE, the graph may contain cycles, chains of nodes which form a closed loop.

Clearly this does not conform at all well to the traditional computer model, so implementations may choose to produce code for a reduction machine of this kind, and then to simulate the reduction machine on a conventional computer. This idea is very similar to familiar interpreted BASIC or Pascal systems, where the source code is translated to an intermediate language which can be regarded as the 'machine code' of an imaginary computer which is simulated by the real machine.

One such scheme uses a graph reduction machine model whose *machine code* is a set of built-in functions called Combinators. This is a very simple scheme which avoids many of the difficulties which can arise in implementing languages which allow functions to be treated as freely as other objects—for example which permit functions to be passed as arguments to other functions and even returned as the value of a function. Readers who have programmed with LISP will be aware of the problems of the scope of names referred to as global variables by LISP functions which occur in conventional *dynamic scoped* LISP dialects and will be familiar with the *function* construct used in some LISP dialects to avoid this *funarg* problem. The Combinator implementation automatically behaves as *static* scoped LISP, but without having to construct *closures* at a run-time to support this behaviour.

EXPRESSIONS, FUNCTIONS AND COMBINATORS

Functional languages are also expression languages, and most allow everyday 'operator' syntax for arithmetical expressions, but to understand how to compile and execute expressions it is easier to work with function applications. Thus

```
2*3+1
```

is really

```
plus (times 2 3) 1
```

where an expression consists of a function name (plus or times in the example), followed by one or more arguments, each of which is either an expression in the same (function application) form, or a constant value.

The reason for adopting this form of expression is that it is easy to store it in a graph. See Fig. 10.1.
Note that in the example the arguments have not been enclosed in parentheses, although one argument is parenthesised to separate its components from the other arguments. The reason for writing

```
plus 2 3
```

and not

```
plus(2,3)
```

is that for some purposes we shall want to think of functions as having only one argument, with plus as a function taking one numeric argument and returning a function which itself takes one numeric argument and returns a value. The value of

```
plus 2
```

is a function that adds 2 to its argument, so that

```
plus 2 3
```

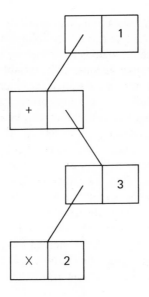

Fig. 10.1

applies the function plus 2 to the argument 3 to obtain the answer 5. Strictly we should parenthesise as

    (plus 2) 3

but we shall assume that function application always associates to the left, so that

    plus 2 3

means

    (plus 2) 3

and not

    plus (2 3)

which is meaningless since 2 is not a function to be applied to an argument 3.

   Now let us turn our expression into a function by defining

    f x <= 2*x + 1

or, in the notation of function application,

    f x <= plus (times 2 x) 1

We can write f 3 as a function application, but when it comes to executing this as a program, we cannot just substitute the body of f for f and still have a form which looks like a function followed by some arguments.

What we are going to do is to find a way of translating function definitions (which look like expressions with variables in some places where a real expression would have a constant), into incomplete expressions so that when completed by adding enough arguments, they actually become expressions in function application form which can be evaluated.

The evaluation strategy is to look at the leftmost function name in the expression: if it is a user defined function then it is replaced by its definition (body) and the result will still be an expression, but if it is a *primitive* function like plus or times, then the indicated operation can actually be performed, (after evaluating the arguments first if necessary, using the same strategy), replacing the function application by its result. In this way the graph becomes *reduced* until no further reductions can be performed, and we should have the value of the original expression as the result.

The translation of function definitions that we are going to undertake takes out references to the functions arguments, a process known as abstraction, and inserts new primitive functions called *Combinators*. The purpose of these is that when they are reduced, they gradually move the actual arguments in the function application into the correct places for their use by the primitive functions like addition. In fact, the reduction has two phases: in the first, the combinator reductions move arguments from their initial positions, finally leaving an expression with no combinators but with all values in place for evaluation of primitive functions in the second phase.

It is time we looked at an example of this translation, and of the reduction process.

It is possible to describe the basic translation very simply using a recursive rule. If we treat all functions as taking only one argument, then every expression either consists of two components, a function and an argument, each of which is also an expression, or of one component, a constant or a variable. We have to give translation rules for these two cases. We shall write

    [x] E

to mean *abstract x from E*. Then, the two component rule can be written as

    [x] (E1 E2) -> S ([x] E1) ([x] E2)

where S is a combinator defined by the reduction rule

    S f g x <= · f x (g x)

The two component rule can be stated as, 'to abstract x from a function application (E1 E2), abstract it separately from each component and prefix the result with a S'.

The one component rule is in two parts

    [x] x -> I
    [x] y -> K y   /* if y is not the same as x */

where

```
I x <= x

K x y <= x
```

Our example

```
f x <= plus (times 2 x) 1
```

proceeds as follows:

```
[x] plus (times 2 x) 1  -> S ([x] (plus
    (times 2 x)) ([x] 1)

[x] 1 -> K 1

[x] (plus (times 2 x)) -> S ([x] plus) ([x]
    (times 2 x))

[x] plus  -> K plus

[x] (times 2 x) -> S ([x] (times 2)) ([x] x)

[x] x -> I

[x] (times 2) -> S (K times) (K 2)
    /*skipping a few steps*/
```

Putting this together we get

```
[x] plus (times 2 x) 1 ->

S (S (K plus) (S (S (K times) (K 2)) I)) (K 1)
```

This is unnecessarily long, and we can find some ways to shorten it. We can observe that

```
S (K E1) (K E2)  = K (E1 E2)
```
and

```
S (K E) I  = E
```

Let us convince ourselves of the first rule by applying both sides to an arbitrary argument x.

```
S (K E1) (K E2) x ->  K E1 x (K E2 x)
            /*by the rule for S*/

K E1 x  -> E1
            /*by the rule for K*/

K E2 x  -> E2
```

so

```
    K E1 x (K E2 x) -> E1 E2
```

but

```
    K (E1 E2) x  -> E1 E2     /* by the rule for K*/
```

Both sides give the same result when applied to any argument, and we can conclude that they are equal.

Making these simplifications to our example abstraction gives

```
    [x] plus (times 2 x) 1 ->
    S (S (K plus) (times 2)) (K 1)
```

We can make further simplifications by introducing two new combinators, B and C, defined by

```
    B f g x  <= f (g x)

    C f x y  <= f y x
```

and introduce them when certain forms occur in the expression.

```
    S (K E1) E2  = B E1 E2

    S E2 (K E2)  = C E1 E2
```

Again we could prove that these equations hold by applying each side to an arbitrary argument and reducing.

With B and C in use, our example simplifies to

```
    [x] plus (times 2 x) 1 -> C (B plus (times 2)) 1
```

Now we can look at the reduction process by applying our function f to an actual argument, say 3.

```
f 3
->
C (B plus (times 2)) 1 3 /* replacing f by its body*/
->
B plus (times 2) 3 1     /*by reduction rule for C*/
->
plus (times 2 3) 1       /*by reduction rule for B*/
```

The first phase is now complete, with no combinators remaining in the expression, and the argument in the right place for evaluation. Now we can reduce plus, but first we must evaluate its arguments. One of them is already a number, but the other is an expression and must be evaluated. Actually we could still have combinators in argument expressions at this stage, so evaluating arguments is exactly the same process as reducing the outer expression.

Once the arguments have been evaluated we can apply the built-in function `plus` to the results and obtain (from `plus 6 1`) a final numeric result 7.

Functions of more than one argument can be translated by abstracting one variable at a time. Since the code produced is fairly lengthy, implementors sometimes introduce some extra combinators, `S'`, `B'` and `C'` defined by

```
S' k f g x <= k (f x) (g x)
B' k f g x <= k f (g x)
C' k f x y <= k (f y) x
```

which have the effect of making the code more compact.

We have now completed a first look at the combinators required to abstract variables from expressions.

MORE ADVANCED LANGUAGE FEATURES

In the following sections we shall look at conditionals, recursion, local definitions, data structures, and pattern matching.

Conditionals

We have seen that some operations must be built-in to the hardware or simulator that runs the combinator code. The arithmetic operators, the comparison operators and the combinators themselves are examples. We also need a conditional operator for translating `if..then..else...` in expressions. We shall choose `cond`, so that `cond x y z` is reduced by testing x, replacing `cond x y z` by y if x evaluates to `true` and by z if x evaluates to `false`.

In the description so far, a particular evaluation strategy has been tacitly assumed, that is, that arguments of functions are not evaluated until their values are actually needed. An alternative strategy always evaluates all arguments to functions before beginning to reduce the function body. In an implementation on a single processor it makes sense to postpone evaluation for as long as possible, in case it turns out that the evaluation is never needed, but in a parallel computer like ALICE, it makes sense to take advantage of spare processing elements to evaluate all arguments so that the minimum of waiting occurs for argument evaluation when they are needed.

We shall return to this subject later, but for the present we should note two things: that if we adopt a delayed evaluation strategy, any functions which require their arguments to be evaluated must be built-in; and that `cond` requires its first argument to be evaluated, but should not have its second or third argument evaluated until it knows which of them is going to be needed. (Otherwise an expression such as 'if x=0 then 1 else 1/x' would always cause an attempt to divide by zero.)

Recursive Functions

Now we can turn our attention to recursive functions. We use the simple example of the factorial function

```
fact n <= if n=0 then 1 else n * fact (n-1)
```

When n is abstracted from this the resulting graph still contains a reference to fact itself. There are two ways to handle this: we could maintain a table or index to function definitions at run-time, so that all references to fact in program graphs actually reference the table, or we could short-circuit this by having the recursive reference to fact in the fact graph reference the top node in the fact graph, introducing a loop into the graph. Either way shall do, although the ALICE computer does not permit loops in graphs for reasons connected with the way it reclaims storage. As the reduction proceeds, new nodes are needed, and references to others are removed. The reduction machine therefore needs a way to reclaim previously used node space for re-use. This garbage collection can be done in a variety of ways, the simplest of which is to examine all graphs, marking memory nodes referred to, and then scanning the whole of node storage collecting on a free storage list all nodes not marked and unmarking the others. This technique requires an interruption in the reduction process from time to time while garbage is collected. The method used in the ALICE is to keep a count in each node of the number of references to it, adjusting this count whenever the graph changes. Then a node can be released to free storage whenever its reference count becomes zero. Graphs with loops always have a non-zero reference count in every node even though there are no references from outside the graph, and so such structures never become free, which is why ALICE does not create them.

Local Definitions

Some functional languages allow local definitions through syntax using let or where. Sometimes these definitions may be recursive, although some languages do not allow this.

Let us begin with a simple, non-recursive example.

```
if x = 0 then 1 else 1/x
    where x = edigit 1000
```

Assume that edigit is already defined and edigit n is the n-th digit of the decimal expansion of the transcendental number e. Actually, any long involved calculation would do here. If we had written

```
if edigit 1000 = 0 then 1 else 1/(edigit 1000)
```

we might find the long calculation being performed twice, when once would do if we could remember the result after the first calculation. We do not have assignment so we are not free to save the result in a variable for later use, but graph reduction causes the replacement in the graph of an expression by its value. In the first way of writing this expression, the subexpression edigit 1000 occurs only once, and will occur only once in the graph, so that once it has been evaluated it is replaced by its value and any other reference to it gets its value immediately. (This is why the graph may not always be a tree, since two nodes may both contain references to the same node.) In the second way of writing the expression there is no connection between the two calculations and unless the compiler is very clever they will appear as separate parts of the graph which just happen to look the same and will be evaluated separately.

We can see how to compile this local definition of x if we think of the whole expression as being like a function application. Suppose we wrote

```
define f x <= if x = 0 then 1 else 1/x
```

and then applied f to an argument

```
f (edigit 1000)
```

The code for f would result from abstracting x from the body of the definition:

```
f <= [x] (cond (eq 0 x) 1 (div 1 x)) ->
            S ( C ( B cond (eq 0)) 1) (div 1)
```

When we supply an argument to f and start to reduce, the first reduction is an S-reduction which causes the argument to be duplicated. With graph reduction the argument itself will not be duplicated, but an extra reference to it will be created.

The local definition should produce the same code, but without defining a named function f in the process.

It is only a very small step to allow functions to be defined locally in where clauses. For example

```
f 3 + f 4
    where f x <=  sin (3*x)
```

Here, f is the function obtained by abstracting x from sin (3*x), and as before, the whole expression can be thought of as a function of f which is f 3 + f 4, applied to the argument f, that is

```
([f] (plus (f 3) (f 4))) ( [x] (sin (times 3 x)))
```

Local recursive definitions do not create named entries in the table, but there is a way to avoid 'tying a knot' in the graph when compiling them. This involves a new combinator called Y. Unfortunately, a full explanation of the Y combinator requires a lot of theoretical background, which cannot be given here. The main feature of Y is that its reduction rule is

```
Y f -> f (Y f)
```

The presence of this rule in the reduction machine effectively prevents an evaluation strategy where arguments are always evaluated before functions are applied (the *eager evaluation* strategy), as after reducing Y f to f (Y f), the argument Y f would be evaluated, producing f (Y f) again and the process would not stop. The appropriate strategy is lazy evaluation (see the Appendix for a fuller description) so that evaluation only occurs when necessary and only as far as necessary.

Again it is time for an example function. Consider

```
fact 3 + fact 4
     where fact n <= if n=0 then 1 else n * fact (n-1)
```

The code generated is

```
([fact] (plus (fact 3) (fact 4)))

        (Y ( [fact] ( [n] ( cond (eq 0 n) 1
              (times n (fact (subtract 1 n)))))))))
```

This has the same form as the earlier local function definition, with fact being defined by abstracting its argument n from its body, and fact being abstracted from the outer expression as if that were a function of fact with the actual definition of fact supplied as an argument. The extra feature is that fact is also abstracted from its own body, and a Y combinator is inserted.

The general shape of this is

```
([fact] E1) (Y ([fact] E2))
```

where E1 represents the outer expression and E2 the definition of fact.

When this is reduced, we evaluate E1, and whenever fact is needed we use the argument (Y([fact] E2)). This is not yet in a suitable form for use as a function, but if we reduce it using the rule for Y, we get

```
([fact] E2) (Y ([fact] E2))
```

which is the definition of fact except that references to fact within E2 have been abstracted out and replaced by (Y ([fact] E2)).

This definition of fact can be used until an internal reference to fact occurs again, when (Y ([fact] E2)) is found, and reduced once to obtain, as before, a definition of fact with internal references to fact replaced. This process can go on until the argument supplied to fact becomes zero and the recursion stops.

It is possible to have several simultaneous local function definitions which are mutually recursive, that is, refer to each other. An explanation of translating these will have to wait until we have looked at data structures in reduction machines.

DATA STRUCTURES

The earliest functional languages had built-in support for one structured data type, the list or sequence. Example programs were published for appending two lists, reversing a list, mapping a function into each member of a list, etc.

A modern language such as Hope also supports user defined structured data types like trees, through its data statement. These types are based on the ability to define constructors, which are like functions in that they have a name and may take a number of arguments, but have no definition, no reduction rule. The idea is that when one of these is encountered in a place where ordinarily reduction would occur, no reduction can take place because there is no rule, and the data item consisting of the constructor and its arguments is itself the result. It will be necessary to evaluate any arguments that are referred to outside the structure. (See Chapter Two for a thorough description of Hope.)

Components of data structures may themselves be objects of the same type, that is, data types may be recursively defined. One result of this is that a list or a tree, for example, may be of potentially infinite extent. Programming with infinite structures may seem strange, but it works if the evaluation strategy is lazy, not evaluating members of data structures before or further than necessary. Some languages associate laziness with the constructor, and do lazy evaluation with some constructors in an otherwise eager evaluation.

Combinator based implementations of data structures are new. Most implementations of functional languages using combinators have only had lists, and have included built-in constructor combinators P (like LISP's cons) which forms a list from an element and a list by adding the element to the front, and nil, which has no arguments and represents the empty list. These languages have also had built-in functions for selecting the arguments of P, called perhaps *head* and *tail* (LISP *car* and *cdr*) and tests to identify the constructors (*iscons* and *isnil*).

If user defined types are to be permitted, a way has to be found to provide all this machinery. Fortunately, this can be done without special functions for each type. First there has to be a way of recognising a constructor. If a table of definitions is kept at run-time, this can indicate the status of a name. Otherwise we need a special combinator with perhaps the constructor name as its first argument, and the rest of the constructor's arguments following. For simplicity, we shall assume the first option.

We also need a way of taking apart the data item, so that its components can be used individually as separate arguments to functions. For this we shall introduce a new combinator U, with the reduction rule

```
U constructor f (constructor arg1...argn)
-> f arg1...argn
```

if the two constructors are the same, otherwise an error value fail to indicate that we have tried to treat an object of one type as if it were a different type.

This U is a generalised version of the U which is paired with P in languages which support only lists.

It may be useful also to provide generalised selectors to pick out individual arguments of constructors, by defining a new combinator, say X with

```
X i (constructor arg1..argi..argn) -> argi
```

For example, head l would be defined as X 1 l, if l evaluates to a list.

PATTERN MATCHING

We can avoid the need to define special tests for constructors by the use of patterns in function definitions. We can define member for a list either using such tests

```
member x l <= if (isnil l) then false
          else if (iscons l) then
                  if (x = head l) then true
                  else member x (tail l)
          else error
```

or by splitting the definition into sub-rules which are selected if the arguments match a certain pattern.

```
member x nil <= false
member x (cons a y) <= if x=a then true
          else member x y
```

These compile as

```
([x] ( U nil false )
```

and

```
([x] ( U cons ([a]([y]( if a=x then
     true else member x y))))))
```

To see how the second one works, if we evaluate member 1 (cons 2 xx) where xx is a list, after the first phase of reduction we shall have

```
U cons ([a]([y](if a=1 then true else member 1 y)))
     (cons 2 xx)
```

The U will not fail since the constructors are both cons, and the next reduction will leave

```
[a]([y]( if a=1 then true else member 1 y)) 2 xx
```

which reduces to if 2=1 then true else member 1 xx.
If we had tried an argument with a different constructor, the U reduction would have returned fail.

To combine the rules, we need a way of reducing all of them until all but one fail. Special combinators called MATCH and TRY have been used to solve this problem, and the problem where a constant value appears in a pattern argument, as in

```
f 1 <=...
```

Finding an efficient way of ordering the tests to select the right rule in a minimum time is an interesting research problem.

SIMULTANEOUS LOCAL DEFINITIONS

We may find a definition of the form

```
E where
     f <= ...g...
     g <= ...f...
```

with each function body referring to the other.

One way to compile this is to collect the separate local rules together into one rule with a pattern valued argument. We invent a new constructor called E, which has a variable number of arguments, the actual number being the value of the first argument. We then get

```
E where (T 2 f g) <= (T 2 (...g...) (...f...))
```

and compiling this gives

```
U' ([f]([g] E)) (Y (U' ([f]([g]( T 2 (...g...)
      (...f...))))))
```

where U is a version of U with

```
U' f (T n arg1...argn) -> f arg1...argn
```

THE SIMULATOR

How do we represent combinator code as a graph, and how do we evaluate it? If we treat functions as having only one argument, as previously described, we can use a graph structure where nodes have just two branches, the left one for the function, and the right one for its argument. Each branch might point to another function application node, or to a single quantity such as a number, a character, a combinator or perhaps a reference to the table of definitions. We code these in a machine dependent way to make possible rapid recognition of the type of value.

We evaluate by locating a subgraph which consists of a primitive operator (the S combinator, for example) and enough arguments to be able to reduce it. We build a new graph for the result of the reduction, and overwrite the root node of the subgraph by the root node of the new graph, leaving the rest of the original graph unaltered. The node we have overwritten represented a function application. We have replaced it by its value. This is illustrated in Fig. 10.2.

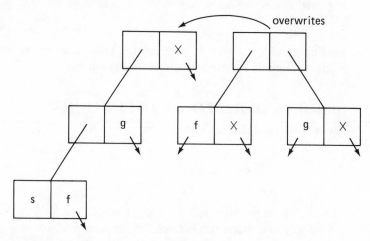

Fig. 10.2

An actual strategy for lazy evaluation on a single processor is as follows. Look down the left branches of nodes until an atom (a single quantity) is found, pushing onto a stack a reference to each node found. If the atom is a function name for a user defined function, keep looking as above, but using the graph for the function body. If the atom is a combinator or built-in function, and all its arguments are present, (they will be pointed to by the top entries on the stack), check to see if any of its arguments must be evaluated before the function can be reduced. If so, call the evaluator recursively for each evaluation. Then perform the reduction, overwriting one node of the graph with the top node of the result as described above. Pop the stack so that its top element refers to the overwritten node and return to the first step.

If the atom is a constructor, no further evaluation is possible. Return the data object as result. If this is the value of an argument to be returned by a recursive call of the evaluator, the caller will take any further action, but if this is the outermost call of the evaluator, and the final result is a structured data object, the top level code must output the result in some suitable format, calling the evaluator for each argument in turn.

Otherwise we may have a quantity like a number or a function with an incomplete set of arguments, (something like plus 1). These are returned to the caller as a result value.

CONCLUSION

What has been described is perhaps the simplest way of implementing a machine for graph reduction. Other schemes have complications with associating values with arguments, which make the implementation more difficult.

The chief disadvantage of the combinator approach is that very large numbers of reductions are needed in solving even quite small problems, and this means that a combinator machine must be very fast indeed to achieve acceptable performance. Some research has been done in looking for new sets of combinators that do more useful work at each reduction step.

What has been learned is that real advantages come from using graph reduction, but that bigger reduction steps, such as are achieved in the ALICE, are essential to the goal of high speed computers to support functional programming.

ACKNOWLEDGEMENT

The original idea for using combinators as an implementation technique for functional programs is due to Prof. David Turner. Much of what is described here was first implemented by him.

11

Ruth: A Runtime System for Hope

Lee McLoughlin and Susan Eisenbach

INTRODUCTION

Ruth was conceived as a run-time system for an implementation of the functional programming language Hope (hence the name—RUn-Time Hope). Ruth was designed to meet two goals—fast execution and support for lazy evaluation. It had to run on conventional machines (The first implementation was on a PDP 11/44) since at the time the hardware dedicated to functional language evaluation was very much in the future. Unfortunately the same statement still applies although many prototype machines exist, and machines dedicated to an almost functional Lisp (assignments are allowed), are commercially available.

On the other hand, Ruth was designed to exploit the capabilities of hardware that is expected to be common—large numbers of processors connected via local area networks. It is hoped therefore that the close correspondence between such conventional hardware and Ruth's architecture will lead to a fast system.

Many of the design decisions in Ruth were heavily influenced by the particular mechanisms used in Hope, so although Hope programs execute quite quickly on Ruth, other languages, even other functional languages, might not fare so well.

SPEED CONSIDERATIONS

Ruth has to evaluate (Hope) programs at a speed that is comparable to existing machines running programs written in a conventional programming language. If this cannot be achieved (via Ruth or any similar system), then functional languages will only ever be useful for prototyping and 'real' programming will continue to use conventional languages. The speed factor becomes even more important in the context of operating system execution, since failure to respond quickly enough (for example when handling hardware interrupts which require acknowledgement within a fixed time), may result in a total failure of the system.

In order to ensure the fast evaluation of programs, certain capabilities common in other (slower) systems are not supported by Ruth:

> (i) Type Checking. There is no way of finding out what a storage cell is being used for. If the programming language requires type checking, then this must be built out of Ruth primitives.
>
> (ii) Ruth does not support multiple classes of storage such as Boolean, integer and string storage classes. The only types provided are integer and task; others have to be mapped onto these.
>
> (iii) Space considerations have been viewed as entirely secondary to speed considerations.

LAZY EVALUATION

The main way the implementation being described differs from other existing Hope systems is that it has entirely lazy semantics (see the Appendix for a description of laziness). The mapping from lazy functions to co-routines is relatively straightforward and many machines provide good support for co-routine evaluation. However, most von Neumann architectures demand explicit programmer control over semaphores or event queues, and the function suspension inherent in lazy evaluation introduces control overheads in addition to the normal access overheads associated with concurrency. In Ruth, semaphore access is incorporated into the basic operand decoding mechanism.

Each co-routine, or task, appears to run in parallel with all other tasks. This is achieved in much the same way that an operating system appears to run several programs in parallel. There is a scheduler which allows each task to execute for a maximum period before the task is forced to suspend itself to allow others a chance to run. Tasks communicate via common memory. This presents a problem in synchronising the access to common memory cells, since the task reading the cell must be suspended until the task which generates the value in the cell has run. In conventional machines this is normally handled with semaphores.

There are two operations a programmer can perform on an initialised semaphore, which can be viewed as an integer variable (s):

> P(s) = Suspend until s > 0, then decrement s.
> V(s) = Increment s.

P can be thought of as an instruction to wait until the semaphore is free; while V makes the semaphore free. Each variable which is to be shared between two or more tasks will have a semaphore associated with it. When a task (the *reader*), tries to read such a variable it must first call P. If the semaphore is free, then the variable has a value and the task can access it. If the semaphore is not free, then the task must wait until a second task (the *initialiser*) initialises the variable and issues a V to free the semaphore. This semaphore governs the *availability* of the variable.

Unfortunately this scheme is too simple to allow for the implementation of lazy evaluation since there is nothing to ensure that the initialiser only begins to execute when a reader attempts to read the variable. In order to achieve this, Ruth provides a second semaphore for every shared variable which governs the *need* for a variable to be initialised. Before attempting to read a value, the reader will issue a V on the need semaphore to allow the initialiser to run. A P is then issued on the avail semaphore to suspend the reader until the value has been generated.

Conversely, the initialiser begins by issuing a P on the need semaphore, suspending its execution until called by a reader. Once the need semaphore is freed, it will restart execution and generate the result before freeing the avail semaphore (with a V) to allow the reader access. Thus:

```
reader:            initialiser:
V(need)            P(need)
P(avail)           write value
read value         V(avail)
```

Note that the term 'initialiser' is used rather than 'writer'. This is because Hope, in common with other functional programming languages, does not allow variables to be updated. Thus once the variable has been initialised, it is permanently flagged as available to all future readers.

In the above scheme need and avail are just simple binary semaphores, which means that they only allow for one reader and one initialiser. However there will generally be multiple readers so the avail semaphore needs to be replaced with an event queue. With the avail semaphore as an event queue when a task calls P on avail, that task is added to the chain of tasks waiting for the event. In this case the event they are waiting for is a call to V on avail. When V is finally called, all the tasks waiting in the chain are allowed to run again.

The need semaphore will only have one task waiting on it (the initialiser) so it does not need to be changed. However, for consistency it too is implemented as an event queue.

To map from a lazily evaluating function to a task, the above synchronisation by the *need* and *avail* events must occur both on the result of the function and on any parameters passed to the function (since these are also shared). In order for both the calling and called functions to refer to the same memory cell, the calling function must allocate space for all the parameters and the result, and pass this to the called function. This is done by means of the Ruth instruction *alloc* which is similar to the 'malloc' library routine available under Unix. The address of the global space returned by alloc is held in space local to the task which called alloc. In Ruth, global store is used solely for communication between functions so that any attempt to read or write a global cell is an attempt to access shared data and must employ the need/avail events. Conversely, if a cell is not global then there are no events associated with it. This is an important design feature of Ruth.

MACHINE DETAILS

Ruth is a three-address machine—the majority of instructions take two source operands and one destination. Each instruction is thirty-two bits long, divided into the four fields as can be seen in Fig. 11.1.

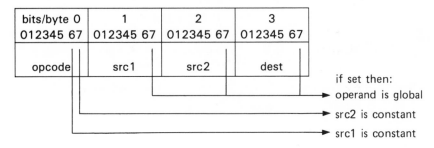

Fig. 11.1

The opcode is held in the first six bits giving a maximum of sixty-four instructions. The remaining two bits in the first byte are used to show whether or not either of the two source operands are constants. (The destination cannot be a constant!) Constants are 8-bit unsigned values. Global addresses are flagged in the last bit in each operand byte.

Global addresses refer to locations in the global store while local addresses are local to the task (i.e. each task is automatically assigned a block of local store). To access a global cell, the instruction must use indirect addressing on the address of the cell which is held in local store. All accesses to cells in global memory must be controlled through the need/avail event mechanism. If the operand is a source, then the *reader* operations are automatically applied to the events associated with the cell, while a global destination will cause the *initialiser* operations to be employed.

Local store is used

(i) to keep (global) addresses of input parameters and that of the function's ultimate result. These addresses are passed by the function invocation mechanism.

(ii) to hold temporary values during the course of calculation—including temporary values of global variables, since these can be accessed much faster from local store than from global store which requires the intervention of the dual event mechanism at each reference.

In a simple Ruth implementation on a conventional machine, the reader operation would be called on the operands in succession. This would mean that the evaluation of the second operand would not begin (i.e. V would not be called on the need event) until the value of the first operand was known. In a multi-processor implementation, this would severely restrict the parallelism so the evaluation of the operands is begun simultaneously (V is called on both need events) although the operands are waited for in succession (i.e. P is called on the avail event of the first operand and only when the value arrives is the second P issued).

So far both global and local memory have been discussed and these are two of the four regions in Ruth's non-uniform memory. The four regions are as follows (see Fig. 11.2):

Regions:

Task   Local   Code   Global

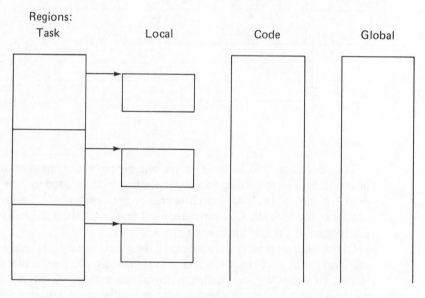

Fig. 11.2

(i) Global Region—accessible to all tasks via need/avail events.

(ii) Code Region—containing code for the user functions. This can be updated only by the system when loading the program. Addresses of functions and instructions in this region are used when calling functions or when executing *goto* instructions respectively.

(iii) Task Region—containing one *Task Control Block* for each task in the system; see Fig. 11.3. The Task Control Block contains all the information (excluding the values of any variables) necessary to start or restart the task. This includes a program counter, the address of the associated local memory, a chain field for when tasks are suspended on queues) and a task status word.

Program Counter
Base Address of Local Memory
Chain Field
Task Status Word

Fig. 11.3

The Program Counter points to the current instruction in the Code Region. It is not updated *until* the instruction has been executed (unlike conventional machines which update the PC after the instruction has been fetched), since instructions may become suspended by the event mechanism. The Task Status Word is used to flag events internal scheduler—like flagging task suspension on a event.

(iv) Local Memory—each task has its own block of local memory. In practice, these blocks are interleaved with the task control blocks to avoid the necessity of maintaining a special base address for each local memory block. With the exception of local memory, all memory addresses within the system are thirty-two bit integers and may be manipulated by means of integer arithmetic. Local memory locations are referenced with seven-bit addresses.

RUTH INSTRUCTION SET

Fig. 11.4 contains a complete set of Ruth's instructions. A description of these instructions follows:

(i) alloc—the first source operand contains the required block size; the second contains a mask value to tell the garbage collector which elements in the block are pointers:

Mask	=	0	>	no pointers;
	=	1	>	all but the first element are pointers;
	=	2	>	first word flags which of the subsequent elements are pointers (max. of 32 pointers).

(ii) free —takes multiple arguments and decrements the reference count of each one. Any reference count which drops to zero will cause the corresponding block to be released to the system.

Operation	Source-1	Source-2	Destination	Description
add	cfg	cfg	fg	
minus	cfg	cfg	fg	
mult	cfg	cfg	fg	
div	cfg	cfg	fg	
rem	cfg	cfg	fg	
and	cfg	cfg	fg	
or	cfg	cfg	fg	
xor	cfg	cfg	fg	
not	cfg		fg	
mv	cfg	fg(offset)		
alloc	cfg	cfg	fg	Alloc a global block
free	f,f,			Garbage Count decrement
gcinc	f			Garbage Count increment
copy	f		f	Copy a global block
cr	f		f	Copy a reference
crt	f	cfg	f	Copy a reference to an offset plus base
crf	f	cfg	f	Copy a reference, offset from a base
need	f			Set need bit
avail	f			Set avail bit
cmp	cfg	cfg	fg	Compare
jmpeq	cfg	cfg	addr	Use result of cmp
jmpeqs	cfg	cfg	addr	
jmpneq	cfg	cfg	addr	
jmpneqs	cfg	cfg	addr	
goto			addr	Unconditional jump
call	addr	f	f,f,--	
calli	addr	f	f,f,--	Call into
callb	f	f		Call bind-block
bindb	addr	f		Create bind-block
bindon	f	f,f,--		Bind argument to bind-block
ret				Return from task

Fig. 11.4   The Ruth Instruction Set

(iii) copy —uses information supplied by alloc to copy block and update reference counters.

(iv) crt, crf —copy instructions. The reference count will be incremented, but the need/avail events on the source and destination operands are not invoked, since this should only occur if the values are being accessed. crt moves the source reference (Src1) to the address given by the sum of the offset (Src2) and the base (Dest). crf moves from the address given by the sum of the source (Src1) and the offset (Src2) to the destination.

(v) The need and avail instructions can be used to force the immediate evaluation of a cell by setting the relevant events for the global cell addressed.

(vi) cmp —compares sources and puts the result into the destination. The result is an integer corresponding to one of the assembler constants

GT, GE, EQ, NE, LE or LT. 'A' is actually a 32-bit Code Region reference which occupies the word following the jump instruction except in the case of the 'short form' jumps (jmpeqs, jmpneqs) in which case the offset is small enough (< 127 words) to fit into the Dest field. goto does not have a separate opcode but is simply a jmpeq with the source operands set equal.

(vii) call—creates a Task Control Block. The program counter is initialised to the value supplied by 'A'. call uses alloc to provide local space for the result (zeroth cell), and for the arguments which follow (up to sixteen arguments allowed). Because 'A' is a 32-bit address, it is stored in the word immediately following the call instruction, and the arguments follow in succeeding words. The return location appears in the Dest field as usual. calli is used to call a function when the return address has already been allocated, and its address is passed in the Dest field. Both call and calli initiate the function which is immediately suspended by a P on the need event of the destination, waiting for a function to require its result.

(viii) bindb, bindon, callb —these are used to implement higher-order functions and Currying (creating new functions by binding arguments to existing ones). bindb allocates a TCB just like call except that a count of the number of arguments already bound is kept (this is called a bind-block). bindon binds the arguments specified in the bind-block created by bindb. callb initiates the function as described in (vii) above.

(ix) ret causes a task to return. Reference counts on all parameters are decremented and the TCB and local store are returned to the system.

GARBAGE COLLECTION

Ruth employs a simple reference count garbage collection scheme. Instructions which cause references to be copied (call, calli, bindb, bindon, callb, cr, crt, crf) will increment the reference counter for the block which the reference addresses. Instructions which cause a reference to be disposed of (ret and free) decrement the reference counter. The alloc instruction initialises the reference counter to one so that as soon as the value drops to zero, the block can be returned to the system. Freeing a block causes all references within that block to be freed. Because of this, certain otherwise valid data types should be avoided—namely self-referential (or circular) types.

SIMPLE DATA TYPES

The basic data types provided in Hope are *num* (the natural numbers and zero), *char* (characters) and *truval* (booleans). Each *num* is stored in a single cell (32-bits). The ordinary arithmetic operations apply. However, because *nums* form a subset of the integers, certain operations may generate values which should cause run-time errors (i.e. negative integers). In Ruth, these underflow errors are not detected since this would slow down program execution quite noticeably.

Characters are also held as integer values (actually the ASCII values). These integers can be compared with each other using cmp, jmpeq and jmpneq instructions. *Truvals* are represented by the integer values zero (false), and one (true). The remaining thirty-one bits are ignored in bitwise logical operations. A considerable amount of space could be saved by representing *chars* as 8-bit values and *truvals* as single bit values but the packing operations required would slow down execution and, as explained earlier, Ruth is implemented for speed efficiency rather than space efficiency.

COMPOUND DATA AND PATTERN MATCHING

In addition to the basic data types, Hope allows programmers to declare their own data types. The simplest user-defined type contains niladic data constructors. In order to differentiate between the constructors, each one is assigned a tag value. These values have to be unique to each constructor in a particular type although, because of the type checking, the same tag values may occur in different types. Thus:

```
data bool == ok ++ not_ok

(tags:        1      2    )
```

A pattern match to detect an ok or a not ok is handled by comparing the value of the tag with constants assigned by the compiler. For example, the guard to match against not ok (i.e. in Hope: ---f (not_ok) <= ... some expression ...) would generate the following instructions (function and functend are inserted by the assembler to aid legibility):

```
f      function
            jmpneq 1.g, 2.c, next_guard
            .. code for the expression ..
            ret
       functend

   next_guard:
```

1.g (first (and only) parameter (global)) is the argument passed to the function, while 2.c (constant, value = 2) is the tag value for not_ok. If the two operands do not match, the code is skipped over and control passes to next_guard.

As well as matching patterns, a guard can also act as a destructor, splitting the data value into its components. For example, a list of numbers may be defined by:

```
data numlist == cons (num, numlist) ++ nil_numlist ;
(tags:            1                      2            )
```

Each element of type numlist may be a cons element and so needs space both for the num and the numlist components. When a new numlist element is needed therefore, alloc is called to create a block large enough for the tag value and the two parameters. If it is known that the element is to be a particular constructor, only enough space is allocated to contain that constructor. Thus only one cell would be required to store the tag value for nil_numlist.

When garbage collecting, the system expects to find the reference count and other information in cells adjacent to, for example, num (this is set up by the alloc instruction). The size of this space cannot be determined by the user program so the value of the num field in cons cannot be stored in the space allocated for the cons itself. Instead, the num field in the cons is used to store a pointer to the actual num. Likewise the numlist component of cons will contain the address of the constructor starting the rest of the list. A numlist element can be seen in Fig. 11.5.

Fig. 11.5

The expression

```
cons (42, nil_numlist)
```

can be seen in Fig. 11.6. Note that nil_numlist is represented by its tag value (2).

A guard to match the cons and break it up into its components

```
(In Hope ---f ( cons ( head, tail )) <= ... some
          expression ...)
```

would be implemented as follows:

```
jmpneq    1.g, 1.c, next_guard    check for cons
crf       1.g, 1.c, 2.f           head is local cell 2
crf       1.g, 2.c, 3.f           tail is local cell 3
...   code for expression ...
ret
next_guard:
```

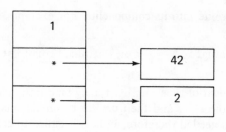

Fig. 11.6

The jmpneq tests the tag value to see if it is a cons cell. If not, then control passes to next_guard. If the tag value matches then the *head* and *tail* components of the expression have to be separated out. This is done by copying the addresses held in the two cells following the tag value into local cells.

The pattern matching scheme described above is not a correct implementation of the semantics of Hope pattern matching. Guards are supposed to be non-overlapping and should therefore be evaluated in parallel. In the current scheme, guards are evaluated sequentially in the same order as they are encountered in the Hope source code. This allows the compiler to be greatly simplified and is in line with other major Hope implementations.

POLYMORPHIC DATA CONSTRUCTORS

Because the individual fields in a data constructor are held as (typeless) pointers—they can address any value or block in global memory regardless of what it contains—polymorphic data constructors are no harder to implement than fixed ones. In the previous example, therefore, the numlist could be generalised to deal with a list of anything, and the compiler would assign tag values and arrange to hold a cons or a nil_value in exactly the same way. The difference between a fixed type list and a polymorphic one lies in the way individual elements of the list are used and not in how they are added to or removed from the list.

LANGUAGE CONSTRUCTS

Expressions

If an expression is given that is not a function call, then it must be converted into a function by the compiler in order to preserve the lazy evaluation semantics. If such a conversion is not performed, the order of evaluation of the program components may change.

Consider the following example:

A Hope fragment might read:

```
let a == 3 + somefun( 4 )
in a + 6
```

This would compile to:

```
        goto      @2
@1      function
        alloc 1.c, 1              reserve space for parameter
        mv    4.c, 1.g,           put the 4 into it
        call  somefun, 2, I       call somefun, the result goes
                                  into 2.g, the parameter is in 1.g
        add   2.g, 3.c, 0.g,      add 3 and put into destination
        ret
@2      alloc 1.c, 1.f
        call  @1, 2, 1
        add   2.g, 6.c, 3.f
```

The expression has been converted into a parameterless function named @1.
If this had not been done and the compiler had simply generated the code
which appears in the function body, then the call to somefun would have
been evaluated before the value of a was required. Converting it into a
function means that the expression will now only be evaluated when a is
needed—i.e. lazily.

Functions

Similarly, if a parameter in a function call involves an expression that is not
simply a variable, a constant or another function call, then the expression
must be converted into a function and the destination for the function passed
instead. A similar process has been called *lambda lifting*.

As an example, consider a call to a function that maps onto a conditional
statement. Only one branch of the actual conditional will be evaluated, so
evaluating both arguments merely to pass them on will alter the semantics
of the program. The only mechanism available in Ruth which can *bundle-
up* an expression and allow a reference to its result to be passed is the function
mechanism. By passing the addresses which are to contain the results of the
functions generated for the two branches of the conditional, the need/avail
event mechanism can be employed to ensure that only the argument which
corresponds to the branch that will ultimately be selected will be evaluated
by the if statement.

Polymorphic Parameters

Like polymorphic data types, polymorphic parameters are effectively indistin-
guishable from ordinary parameters since arguments of both classes are
passed by reference. In a polymorphic function the parameter is either passed
to other functions or used in constructing polymorphic data items. In both
cases only the reference is required and not the actual value it represents.

The sole complication with polymorphic parameters arises when the result of a function is returned, then the size of its result is known to the call instruction which can generate the necessary space to hold a copy of the result. When a single polymorphic parameter is being copied however, its size is not known. To overcome this problem, functions which do this cause a 'relay' address to be generated, and it is the address of this which is inserted into the destination cell generated by the call instruction. The cell can be treated as if it were the result (and not merely a reference to it), until the actual value is required. Once this occurs and the function has been executed, it causes the relay address to point indirectly to the actual result generated. Subsequent attempts to access the cell addressed by the relay cell wil be detected by the Ruth system which, without additional programmer intervention, will make an extra level of indirection to reach the correct result.

CONCLUSION

Ruth is an abstract machine designed to run a lazy version of Hope rapidly. It is a three address machine with a non linear address space, no registers and no stack. Its mechanism for dealing with function calls is the standard operating system tasking model. It is currently implemented on a Whitechapel MG1 and on a High Level Hardware Orion in a single processor version.

Appendix
Lazy Evaluation

In most conventional languages, the value of a function is calculated when the code to handle it is reached. (This is termed 'call by value' since the value, rather than the references, to the parameters are passed.) Lazy evaluation, on the other hand is a call mechanism where the value of the function is only calculated when required. This means that the code which generates the value (the function) must be suspended at the point of call until the result is wanted, and then restarted to generate the value. This suspended function must have access to the environment that was current when it was suspended, and to the values of any variables needed to work out the result.

To illustrate the value of lazy evaluation, consider the following:

```
ttyin
```

is a function which returns a list of characters typed in at the terminal;

```
ttyout
```

takes a list of characters and displays each in turn at the terminal. With call-by-value semantics, the call

```
ttyout ( ttyin )
```

require that the input is completed before any output appears on the screen. With lazy evaluation, on the other hand, each character typed is immediately needed by ttyout which echoes it on the screen. Hope as defined at Edinburgh University and implemented both there and in the Declarative Systems Architecture group at Imperial college, supports lazy evaluation solely to facilitate interactive input/output (it has a single lazy constructor functions (lcons) and no means for the programmer to develop others).

Selected Bibliography

Backus, J., *Can Programming be Liberated from the von Neumann style? A Functional Style and Its Algebra of Programs*. ACM Turing Lecture, *CACM.*, Vol. 21, No. 8, August 1978, pp. 613–641.
The original FP paper which defines the language and introduces some algebraic properties.

Backus J., The Algebra of Functional Programs, Function Level Reasoning, Linear Equations, and Extended Definitions, Springer-Verlag Proceedings, *Formalization of Programming Concepts*, Spain, April 1981, Vol. 107.
Defines linear forms, shows how they may be built up from simpler ones and proves the Linear Expansion Theorem; as well as outlining some possible extensions to FP.

Backus J., From Function Level Semantics to Program Transformation and Optimisation, *Mathematical Foundations of Software Development*, Springer-Verlag, Vol. 185.
Summary of more recent work on FP, in particular, optimization.

Burstall R.M. and Darlington J., A Transformation System for Developing Recursive Programs, *JACM*, No. 1, Vol. 24., Jan 1977.
The seminal paper on the unfold/fold transformation system.

Burstall R.M., MacQueen D.B. and Sannella D.T., HOPE, An Experimental Applicative Language, Proceedings 1980 LISP Conference, Stanford, California, pp. 136–143, Internal Report CSR-62–80, Department of Computing Science, University of Edinburgh, 1980. Updated Feb. 1981.
The original description of the language.

Clark K.L. and Sickel S. Predicate Logic, a Calculus for Deriving Programs, *Proceedings 5th International Joint Conference on Artificial Intelligence*, Vol. 1, 1977.
The application of transformation to logic programming.

Darlington J. The Structured Description of Algorithm Derivations, Invited Paper, International Symposium on Algorithms, Amsterdam, 1981, *Algorithmic Languages*, pp. 221–250. Ed. de Bakker/van Vliet, North-Holland Publishing Co., 1981.
The ideas behind the HOPE meta-language system.

Darlington J., Henderson P. and Turner D.A. *Functional Programming and its Applications, An Advanced Course*, 1981, Cambridge University Press.
An advanced collection of papers including Turner: Recursion Equations as a Programming Language; Williams: Notes on the FP Style of Functional Programming; Guttag: Notes on Using Type Abstractions in Functional Programming; Darlington: Program Transformation; Treleaven: Computer Architecture for Functional Programming.

Darlington J. and Reeve M.J. ALICE, A MultiProcessor Reduction Machine for the Parallel Evaluation of Applicative Languages, *Proceedings ACM Conference on Functional Programming Languages and Computer Architecture*, Portsmouth, New Hampshire, 1981, pp. 166–170.
The original ALICE paper.

Darlington J. and Reeve M.J., ALICE and the Parallel Evaluation of Logic Programs, *Proceedings 10th Annual ACM/IEEE Symposium on Computer Architecture*, Stockholm, 1983.

Dijkstra E.W. *A Discipline of Programming*, Prentice-Hall, 1975.

Glaser H., Hankin C. and Till D. *Principles of Functional Programming*, Prentice-Hall, 1984.
A comprehensive undergraduate level textbook.

Johnsson T. The G-Machine, an Abstract Machine for Graph Reduction, *Proceedings of the Declarative Programming Workshop*, UCL, April 1983.
Contains a description of lambda-lifting, a compilation technique for higher-order functions.

Keller R.M., Lindstrom G. and Patil S., An Architecture for a Loosely-Coupled Parallel Processor, Internal Report UUCS-78–105, Dept. of Computer Science, University of Utah, 1978.

Kieburtz R.B. and Shultz J., Transformation of FP Program Schemes, *Proceedings ACM Conference on Functional Programming Languages and Computer Architecture*, 1981.
Discusses transformation, in particular recursion removal, via algebraic manipulation.

Partsch H. and Steinbruggen R., A Survey of Program Transformation Systems, *Journal ACM Computing Surveys*, Vol. 15, No. 3, September 1983.
A comprehensive survey of transformation systems.

Pepper P., Program Transformation and Programming Environments, Springer Verlag, Proceedings Workshop directed by F.L. Bauer and H. Remus, 1984.
An accessible introduction to many of the strands of transformation work under way at present.

Teitelman, W., *INTERLISP Reference Manual*, Xerox PARC, 1974.
Lists the facilities available to an INTERLISP user.

Treleaven P.C., Brownbridge D.R. and Hopkins R.P., Data-Driven and Demand-Driven Computer Architecture, *Journal ACM Computer Surveys*, Vol. 14, No. 12, March 1984.

Turner D.A., A New Implementation Technique for Applicative Languages, *Journal Software, Practice and Experience*, Vol. 9, 1979.
A description of compiling the functional language SASL to combinators.

Turner D.A., The Semantic Elegance of Functional Languages, *Proceedings ACM/MIT Conference on Functional Languages and Computer Architecture*, Portsmouth, Massachussetts, 1981.

Vegdahl S.R., A Survey of Proposed Architectures for the Execution of Functional Languages, *Journal IEEE Transactions on Computers*, Vol. C–33, No. 12, December 1984.

Welsh, J., Elder, J. and Bustard D., *Sequential Program Structures*, Prentice-Hall International, London, 1984.
This book describes Pascal-Plus and abstract data types.

Yourdon E., *Techniques of Program Structure and Design*, Prentice-Hall, 1975.
A classic systems analysis book.

Index